Vardon in 1899 (29 years old) at the peak of his game.

THE CLASSICS OF GOLF

Edition of

VARDON ON GOLF

Compiled and Edited by

Herbert Warren Wind

and

Robert Macdonald

Foreword by Herbert Warren Wind
Afterword by S. L. McKinlay

Acknowledgement

This book was the idea of Susan Lewis, a distinguished rare-golf-book dealer, a member of a hardy species who has endured a long winter but sees ahead a warm and brilliant spring.

Foreword

Harry Vardon was the best golfer of his day, and his day lasted a long time, from 1896, when he won the first of his six British Open championships, through 1920, when he finished in a tie for second in our Open, at Inverness, in Toledo, a stroke off the pace. He was fifty then, and his near-miss could be likened to a contemporary golfer of over sixty barely failing in his quest for a major championship.

Vardon's longevity underlines vividly that he was as accomplished a golfer as ever lived. A pleasant, equable, and foursquare man who, along with John Henry Taylor and James Braid, formed the Great Triumvirate at the turn of the century when golf enjoyed a prodigious leap into world prominence, Vardon compiled a list of achievements that is staggering. At this writing, he is the only golfer who has won the British Open six times. He popularized the overlapping grip, which is used by ninety-nine per cent of the world's golfers. His simplified, upright backswing was a revolutionary step forward from the overly long and Laocoönish St. Andrews backswing that had hitherto been regarded as the last word in style. His three American tours—in 1900, 1913, and 1920—had a great deal to do with the swift rise in golf's popularity on these shores. It is small wonder that, whenever the Ryder Cup match is contested in Great Britain, it has long been traditional for the American team to make a pilgrimage to Vardon's grave in Totteridge, north of London, where he was the professional at the South Herts Golf Club at the time of his death in 1937.

Since Vardon was such an amiable man, it is odd that a number of stories about him picture him as terse and

amusingly undiplomatic. For example, during his Amer-
ican tour in 1913 with Ted Ray, the 1912 British Open
champion, they played a four-ball match in Chicago
against a local professional and a left-handed amateur
who put up a very good fight. The amateur, who had shot
the best round of his life, was bent on extracting a word of
praise from the great man and asked Vardon who was the
best left-handed golfer he had ever encountered. "Never
saw one who was worth a damn," Vardon replied. In the
1920 United States Open at Inverness, the United States
Golf Association thought that it might add something to
the occasion if Vardon was paired in the qualifying
rounds with Bobby Jones, the eighteen-year-old Ameri-
can whiz. On the seventh hole, a short par 4, Jones, trying
to spin a niblick pitch close to the hole, skulled the ball
yards over the green and ended up by taking a bogey 5.
"Mr. Vardon, did you ever see a worse golf shot than
that?" Jones asked in embarrassment as they walked off
the green after holing out. "No," Vardon answered. I
bring these incidents up, as I say, because they are so
untypical of Harry Vardon. It was not just the superb
shotmaking of Vardon, Taylor, and Braid but also their
admirable manners and character that brought golf its
immense new popularity.

Vardon looms as an intensely fascinating figure. Born
on the island of Jersey in 1870, he was the son of a gar-
dener. More likely than not he would have followed in his
father's footsteps had a group of young English golfers not
arranged with the authorities in the village of Grouville to
lay out a golf course over the common land in 1877.
Vardon learned the game as a caddie and went on to play
it well, but in his early teens he was apprenticed as a
gardener to a retired army officer. He might well have
spent his life pulling out weeds and planting annuals
save for the enterprising nature of one of his younger
brothers, Tom. Aware that golf was booming in England

and that there were jobs in it to be had there, Tom found employment at the club in St. Anne's-on-Sea, the first step in a most successful career that saw him contend on several occasions in the British Open and eventually to cross the Atlantic and become the head professional at important golf clubs in the American Mid-West. It was Tom who secured Harry his first job in golf, at Ripon in England, and who watched over him until he made his mark by winning the British Open at Muirfield in 1896.

After his breakthrough in the British Open, Vardon continued to refine his shotmaking skills and to gain an increasing confidence. In winning the British Open in 1898 and 1899, he showed himself to be in a class by himself as a striker of the gutta-percha golf ball, the ball that had replaced the old feather ball midway through the century. Few of his contemporaries were as long or as straight off the tee, and on lengthy holes none of his rivals could match his sweeping brassie second shots that covered the flag. Hit with perfect underspin, the ball would pull up quickly upon landing on the green and finish ten to fifteen feet from the flagstick. Had his putting been as brilliant as his play from tee to green, the record-breaking scores he brought in would have been even more awesome, but Vardon was merely a good putter, not a genius on the greens like Willie Park, Jr.

Shortly after the turn of the century, Vardon's position as the dominant player in golf was rocked by two unforeseen developments. The first was the introduction of the rubber-cored ball. Vardon continued to be one of the game's top shotmakers, but he was never quite as much at home with the rubber-cored ball as he had been with the gutty, and his writing is replete with mournful allusions to the superior game golf had been. However, he won his fourth British Open with the rubber-cored ball in 1903, and won it by six strokes. Then, at the tail end of that season, he suffered a really terrible blow. He came down with a serious illness that made it necessary for him to enter a sanatorium in Mundesley, in Norfolk. In his books Vardon never stated the nature of his illness, but it was tuberculosis. He resumed playing tournament golf the following season, but was forced to return to Mundesley several times in the years ahead. He managed, however, to remain at the forefront of the game until the 1920s, although he was never again quite the amazing player he had been at the turn of the century.

A word about the format of "Vardon on Golf." It is a composite of individual chapters and other material selected at random from four books Vardon wrote: "The Complete Golfer," published in 1905; "How To Play Golf," published in 1912; "Progressive Golf," published in 1920; and "My Golfing Life," published in 1933. Henry Leach, a well-known golf writer, worked with Vardon on "The Complete Golfer", but we do not know who were his collaborators on his other books. They shared a tendency to be prolix, a fondness for complicated sentences, and a weakness for rambling on about inconsequential matters. Accordingly, we have taken the privilege of editing the material substantially in order to make it clearer, crisper, and more pleasant to read. A series such as The Classics of Golf would be incomplete if it did not present the reader with a chance to get to know Harry Vardon, who ranks alongside Bobby Jones, Ben Hogan, and Jack Nicklaus in the top echelon of the game's great champions.

The Table of Contents explains the format of "Vardon on Golf." Part I consists of the first six chapters of "My Golfing Life." They cover Vardon's youth on Jersey; his tentative first years as a professional; his emergence as a champion in the 1896 British Open; his excellent golf in winning the British Open at Prestwick in 1898 and at Sandwich in 1899, and his triumph over Willie Park, Jr., in 1899 in their highly publicized challenge match over seventy-two holes; his successful American tour in 1900 *during which he won the United States Open at the Chicago Golf Club; his fourth victory in the British Open at Prestwick in 1903; and his illness at the end of the season that forced his retirement to the sanatorium in Mundesley. Part V of "Vardon on Golf" returns to "My Golfing Life", picking up the narrative in 1904 when he rejoined the professional golf circuit. We follow Vardon's gradual return to the top rung of the game: his fifth victory in the British Open in 1911 at Sandwich after a playoff with Arnaud Massy; his long-overdue success in the British Professional Match-Play Championship; the memorable three-way playoff in the 1913 United States Open in which Vardon and Ted Ray opposed Francis Ouimet at The Country Club, near Boston; Vardon's record sixth victory in the British Open in 1914 at Prestwick; and his gallant effort in 1920 to win our Open at Inverness, the last tournament of consequence in which he was a factor.*

In "Vardon on Golf," Part I and Part V are wrapped around Parts II, III, and IV. Part II is a series of topnotch instruction chapters from "The Complete Golfer." It includes Vardon's shrewd advice to beginners; the value of the overlapping grip; the primary role he assigns to learning how to hit the drive correctly; the beginner's progress from the driver to the brassie and the cleek, two clubs that Vardon played exceedingly well; and his description of the push shot, the iron shot that set the master golfers apart from the others in the era of the gutta-percha ball. The hand action required to the play the push shot is evident today in the skills of the best modern shotmakers.

Part III is a chapter on putting taken from "How to Play Golf." Part IV, another chapter on putting, appeared in "Progressive Golf." After Vardon's illness, short putts were the bane of his existence. He never knew when a nerve in his right arm would jump before he struck the ball with his putter. Both of these pieces are light, meandering essays in which Vardon reveals himself as a man who had an extensive knowledge of putting, that game within a game. When he refers to himself as a player who was regarded as an able approach putter, he is indulging in arrant understatement. The other day I happened to run across a report on Vardon's gala season in 1898, which H.S.C. Everard wrote for Badminton magazine. After saluting Vardon's command of the driver and the brassie, Everard remarks, "This in the course of a day's play will tell its own tale; especially as Vardon, once on the green, has such an unrivalled knowledge of strength that time after time he lays his first putt within three inches of the hole, thus leaving himself far less than his due proportion of shortish, but withal missable, putts to hole out."

S.L. McKinlay has written a splendid Afterword for "Vardon on Golf" in which, among other things, he reaches back and remembers watching Vardon play at a Victory Tournament put on by the Glasgow Golf Club at its course in Killermont in 1919. Sam McKinlay, a member of the British Walker Cup team in 1934, was a journalist by profession. He wrote everything from incisive editorials to thoughtful golf columns for the Glasgow Herald, the morning newspaper published by the George Outram organization, along with a wide diversity of reports and articles for the Glasgow Times, the Outram evening paper. Near the end of his career, McKinlay was the editor of the Times. He somehow managed to find the free moment to contribute golf reports and essays to British and American periodicals. McKinlay's sound judgment of players and courses went hand in hand with a style that was always perceptive and frequently inspired, and it is a considerable loss to golf literature that his work was not periodically collected into books.

I believe it was McKinlay's habit during his palmy days as a golfer to take his annual vacation from work when the British Amateur was scheduled to be played. With far *less practice than ninety per cent of the field, over the years McKinlay managed to reach every round of the Amateur except the final. He had a wonderfully natural swing with more than a touch of Jones in it.*

Herbert Warren Wind

VARDON ON GOLF

A Collection of Harry Vardon's
Writings on the Game

HOW "VARDON ON GOLF" IS ORGANIZED

TABLE OF CONTENTS

Illustrations

Vardon in 1899 at the peak of his game. THE BADMINTON MAGAZINE.

The young Vardon working on his game. MY GOLFING LIFE.

Vardon's first big success. ROYAL PORTRUSH GOLF CLUB.

J.H. Taylor, the first of the Great Triumvirate to win the British Open. ILLUSTRATED LONDON NEWS PICTURE LIBRARY.

The Ganton football team. MY GOLFING LIFE.

North Berwick: the end of the day's play. MY GOLFING LIFE.

Ganton: Park putting but Vardon in charge. MY GOLFING LIFE.

The carry from the eighteenth tee at Ganton. THE GOLF COURSES OF THE BRITISH ISLES.

Vardon with Alex Finlay. MY GOLFING LIFE.

Vardon returns to Britain. ILLUSTRATED LONDON NEWS PICTURE LIBRARY.

Vardon in 1900 after winning the American Open. ATTRIBUTION UNKNOWN.

My set of clubs. THE COMPLETE GOLFER.

The stance for the driver and brassy. THE COMPLETE GOLFER.

The overlapping grip. THE COMPLETE GOLFER.

The top of the swing. THE UNITED STATES GOLF ASSOCIATION MUSEUM AND LIBRARY.

The finish. MY GOLFING LIFE.

The finish of a push shot. MY GOLFING LIFE.

The Great Triumvirate. FROM THE PAINTING BY CLEMENT FLOWER.

Vardon and Braid tee off at St. Andrews. MY GOLFING LIFE.

The eighteenth green: the playoff of the 1913 American Open. THE UNITED STATES GOLF ASSOCIATION MUSEUM AND LIBRARY.

Vardon at Prestwick in 1914. MY GOLFING LIFE.

Taylor picks up another stroke. MY GOLFING LIFE.

Vardon, fifty, paired with Jones, eighteen. UNITED STATES GOLF ASSOCIATION MUSEUM AND LIBRARY.

Vardon, in top form. UNITED STATES GOLF ASSOCIATION MUSEUM AND LIBRARY.

PART I
FROM "MY GOLFING LIFE"

This stone slab was erected to mark Harry Vardon's birthplace in the town of Grouville in Grouville Parish on the Channel island of Jersey. The house bordered the Gory common land behind the Bay of Grouville where the Royal Jersey golf course was first laid out in 1877 when Harry was seven years old.

The Gory Village school in the Parish of Grouville where Harry Vardon was taught by Mr. Boomer, father of champion golfer, Aubrey Boomer, and legendary golf teacher, Percy Boomer. In addition to Harry, Mr. Boomer taught many other excellent golfers: Harry's brothers, Tom and Alfred, the three Gaudins, Renouf, and Ted Ray.

LEARNING THE GAME
ON THE ISLAND
OF JERSEY

I was born on May 9th, in the year 1870, at the little town called Grouville, which is a few miles from St. Helier on the island of Jersey. My parents were both natives of Jersey, and my father was a gardener there all his life. We were a large family, consisting of seven boys and two girls. My brothers, George, Phil, and Edward, all came before me, Tom and Fred coming after in that order.

It appears to have been generally accepted that my brother Tom, who was the professional to the Royal St. George's Club at Sandwich for many years, and who has been in America for some considerable time, was my senior. This, however, is not the case. My youngest brother Fred is also a professional, and was for many years located at Weston-super-Mare. Fred started his career as my assistant when I was at Ganton. His first professional appointment was to the Filey Golf Club in Yorkshire and later he occupied the same position at Biggleswade, Herts.

I had always thought Fred would turn out to be the best golfer in the family. He was a fine natural player. That he did not fulfill my expectations has been a source of regret to me.

Mr. Boomer, the father of those two fine golfers, Aubrey and Percy, was the schoolmaster at the village school in Gory which we all attended. I am sorry to say that learning had little attraction for me in those youthful days, and my old schoolmaster had certainly no reason to be proud of me at that time. Schooling was very different at this period from what it is today. Our parents paid the sum of twopence a week for each of us to attend the school, and both my brother Tom and myself were guilty on many occasions of playing truant. The one subject more than any other which I disliked was the lessons in French. Whenever it was possible to do so, we would spend the school fee on something more enjoyable than French. I particularly remember that at the arithmetic lessons Mr. Boomer, for some reason or other, always placed me at the head of the class. It was not long, however, before I was at the other end, and it was perhaps only right that I was considered the dunce of the school. I recall, on one occasion, when I had hastily passed from the top to the bottom of the class, that Mr. Boomer told me to go and clean out his rabbit hutch. To some boys this might have served as a punishment, but to me it was a happy release. Anything in the nature of activity appealed to me far more than the acquiring of knowledge. I was as enthusiastic as it was possible to be in any games that were played, and one of my first ambitions was to excel at cricket. I retained my liking for this fine sport all my life and played often in my later years.

It was when I was about seven years of age, in the year 1877, that the event which was eventually to map out my career for me came to pass. The people of Grouville lived a quiet, undisturbed life, and had, as is usual with those who live a somewhat uneventful existence, a whole-hearted respect for the sanctity of the Sabbath Day. It so happened, however, that this should be the very day which a small party of strange gentlemen selected to make their appearance on the common land. They brought with them instruments with which to survey and mark out places for tees and greens. The story that preparations were being made to play a game called golf was soon spread about the village. The indignation of the tenant farmers was quickly aroused, and they thought out and discussed every possible means by which they could expel these trespassers from the common land. Indignation spread through Grouville, and these golfers were regarded in anything but a friendly light. Having obtained the necessary authority and permission from the constable of the parish, their position was quickly made secure, and from that day a new feature entered into our lives. The natural state of the land was so perfect that little work needed to be done, and possibly no good golf course was ever so easily made. The grass was short and springy as it is on all good sea coast links. Sand was plentiful and natural hazards were everywhere. The grass was of such splendid texture that it was only necessary to put the mower and roller over the selected space and superior putting greens were made. I have, personally, supervised and laid out many golf courses during my career as a professional golfer, but never have I seen a first-class course so easily designed. A little inn close by was immediately renamed the Golf Inn. Thus the headquarters of the Jersey golfers was established. That in brief was the start of the Royal Jersey Golf Club.

The links when they were completed proved to be excellent, better in fact than they are today. One of the chief reasons for this is that most of the bunkers have since been filled with clay, which spoiled them. It was necessary to do this to prevent the sand from them being blown over the course by the strong winds which frequently sweep across the island. When everything was in readiness for play, many golfers came over from England to enjoy this, to us, new game.

I was first introduced to golf along with many other boys my age. We were enticed to carry the clubs of the visitors. As far as I can remember we did not think very much of this new game, but after carrying a few times we began to see possibilities in it. It was only natural that we should wish to try our hand at playing ourselves. This, however, was not so easily done. There were many difficulties to be overcome. Apart from not having any links on which to play, we had no clubs or balls. So keen, however, were we to play that these difficulties were eventually solved. As a start, we laid out our own course, consisting of four holes, each about fifty yards in length and for boys of our age quite good enough. When we had marked out and made our teeing grounds and smoothed out the greens, there next came the question of balls, and in the absence of real gutties we decided the most suitable article for us was the big white marble, which we call a taw, and which was about half the size of an ordinary golf ball. The question of clubs was a more difficult proposition, and caused a good deal of anxiety in our young minds. On reflection, I think great credit is due to us for the manner in which we solved this problem. As nothing would be really satisfactory except a club which resembled a real golf club, it was necessary to make many experiments before we were able to get the desired article. As a start, we decided that we must use as hard a wood as possible, and the wood from a tree which we called the "Lady Oak" was suitable for our purpose. First of all, we cut a thick branch from the tree, sawed off a few inches from it, trimming this piece as near as we possibly could to the shape of the heads of the drivers of those players for whom we had been carrying. As splicing was impossible, it was agreed that we must bore a hole in the centre of the head. This we did with a red-hot poker. The shaft sticks were made of thorn, white or black, and when they had been trimmed and prepared, we proceeded to fit them into the holes. Then after tightening them with wedges, the operation was complete. All things considered, we were able to hit a long ball with this primitive driver. After a time, as we grew more accustomed to making these clubs, we became quite expert young club makers. The brassies seen on the links had made a big impression upon us, and as we had experienced some trouble with our oak heads—since they were green, they were rather inclined to crack—we eventually decided to sheathe the heads entirely with tin. This was not an easy thing to do, and we were further handicapped by the fact that our fathers declined to lend us their tools, and we had to "borrow" them when the proper occasion presented itself.

These tin-plated drivers, which we called our brassies, were an enormous improvement over our original clubs. So expert did we become at making them that occasionally one would stand out as far superior to the others. The reputation of the maker of this club was assured, and he did a good business in making clubs for others. A big price in marbles was demanded and paid to this expert club maker.

We played our elementary kind of golf whenever possible. I recall that most of our best games took place in the moonlight, which was exceedingly bright in Jersey, and enabled us to see quite well. We arranged competitions on the medal system by scores, and frequently got threes at our fifty-yard holes. With our home-made clubs and little white taws, coupled with our lack of knowledge and extreme youth, I can truthfully say that our efforts were very creditable. This was my introduction to the game of golf.

As time went on, we began to carry more and more for the players who visited Grouville and soon were able to find real balls. Occasionally, too, we had one given to us, along with a club, normally a damaged one, which we repaired. Usually, a new shaft was needed, and we put in the sticks, as we had done with the clubs of our own make, by burning holes in the heads. Sometimes, as a reward, a golfer for whom we had often carried would give us an undamaged club. This indeed was a big event in our young lives, and the proud possessors were looked up to by those who had not been so fortunate.

There were some very good golfers who came to play over the Jersey links. I recall in particular a Dr. Purviss who was well known in golf and who always said, in after years, that he was the only one to teach me golf. As was natural for boys, we watched the good golfers closely, and, being natural mimics, copied what we saw.

The Vardons were a large family, and it was necessary for us boys to do something which would contribute to the family funds. I only carried clubs about twice a week and spent many hours on the beach, collecting seaweed which, when sold, brought in quite a nice sum. As I have previously stated, I was not much good at school, but I can truthfully claim that I was not an idle boy. I worked and worked hard throughout my youthful days—on reflection, I feel sure the work I was forced to do in my youth helped to prepare me for the many adverse circumstances which must befall any young man when he starts out in the battle of life.

At about the age of twelve I went to work on a farm. My duties there were numerous, and I had very little time to spare for golf. I lived on the farm and, apart from making butter and doing other odd jobs, it was my task to work the pump which was used as a cooler for the milk urns. A year or two later, I entered the service of a Doctor Godfrey, and for three or four years had practically no golf at all. It is true that occasionally I would go out on a moonlight night and play with some of the other boys, but these games were few and far between. I was given a half holiday about twice a year, and I looked forward to them mightily. It was on these precious days that I used to play golf with my brother Tom, and I remember I was nearly always able to beat him. I mention this fact in no spirit of boasting, but only because a few years later it had a profound bearing on my future life. My duties with Dr. Godfrey consisted of waiting at table and acting as page boy. Occasionally, when the doctor drove his trap to visit a patient, he would require me to accompany him in order to have someone to mind the horse during his absence. However much I might have wished to do so, I had little time to give to golf. In later years, many people have said to me, "I used to know you when you were playing golf as a boy in Jersey." Actually it was my brother Tom they knew. He played a good deal of golf.

The years were passing, and my ambition was to be-

come a gardener. At the age of seventeen, I went to Major
Spofforth's estate—and a very beautiful place it was too—
to learn gardening. The Major was a keen golfer, and
occasionally took me out to play with him. He gave me
some of his old clubs, a source of joy to play with after the
clumsy home-made ones I had always used. I remember
distinctly the old yellow driver which was a great favourite of mine. In those days the wooden clubs were nearly
always stained a light colour. Today, the dark stain appears to be more popular.

Although I have always been called "Harry", I was
christened Henry. At home it was always "Harry", but
Major Spofforth called me by the name I was christened
with. He gave me, along with the prized yellow driver, an
iron. This club, which in my eyes was almost as valuable
as my driver, was used for all types of strokes, even being
brought into service as a putter. These were the days
when any type of putt had no terrors whatsoever for me,
and I can honestly say that my work on the greens was all
that could be desired. Maybe there are many people who,
having witnessed some of my poorer exhibitions of holing
out, will be surprised to read this. The fact remains, however, that, until after my serious illness and the advent of
the rubber-cored ball, my putting never gave me any
cause for anxiety.

As regards my grip, I can only say that I utilized the
same method which was universal with most golfers at
that period, namely, the two-handed palm grip. My
swing was, as far as I can recall, something in the nature
of what it always has been. Many critics of the game have
commented on the fact that all Jersey-born golfers
adopted the upright swing in the days when the flatter
method, known as the St. Andrews swing, was universal.
There is some mystery as to why we Jersey players hit
upon this method in preference to the other. Possibly it
was that we just naturally took the club up to the top by

the shortest route. Whatever the cause, such well-known Jersey players as my brother, Tom, Ted Ray, the Gaudins, the Becks, and the Renoufs, and, in later years, the Boomers, all swung their clubs in this manner.

I enjoyed an occasional round without in any way aspiring to any big success on the links. As a matter of fact, I enjoyed other sports just as much, if not more so, than golf—cricket and football, for example. I was also extremely fond of running. I went in for all kinds of races, obstacle, flat, and hurdle. I think my best distance was 150 yards, and I recall that I won many prizes at this sprinting distance. I remember very clearly during a holiday taking part in six races in two days. Willie Gaudin and I used to train together on the common. Gaudin, who later on was to become a well-known golfer, was the professional at Bradford in Yorkshire for many years, and afterwards went to America.

However, to get back to golf, the occasional rounds which I played with Major Spofforth were the extent of my participation in the game. A rather curious feature of these matches occurs to me as I write. I can truthfully assert that when I had taken up professional golf as a means of livelihood, I never suffered from nerves. In fact, I did not know what it was to be nervous in any golfing event in which I took part throughout my golfing career. However, in all these early games, I was exceedingly nervous. Why, I do not know. It is certain that nothing important depended on the result.

While working as gardener for Major Spofforth I had joined a Working Men's Club, which had been formed. About this period, I had started to play reasonably well. My handicap at the club was plus 3, but I would not have been that low in any other club. On reflection, I should think that I played to about a handicap of eight. It was during the time that I was a member of this club that I won my first prize. I came very near to losing my cherished trophy when the German airmen visited North London in one of their raids during the Great War. A bomb was dropped at the door of my home at Totteridge, which brought part of the building down and severely damaged, among other things, this valued prize of mine—but happily not beyond repair. Anyhow I was by then about twenty years of age, and I have often recalled the words which my employer spoke to me one day after we had finished playing a round. Although it is over forty years ago now, I can hear him saying, "Henry, my boy, never give up your golf, it may be useful to you one day." My younger brother Tom had already left Jersey and gone to St. Anne's-on-Sea to learn club-making from Lowe. Very soon after his departure, an event was to occur which was to change the whole course of my life. I had just recently been married, and news reached me that my brother had won second prize in an open professional tournament at Musselburgh in Scotland. His prize amounted to twelve pounds ten shillings, a sum which to me in those days appeared to be a fortune. Wages were counted in shillings in Jersey at that time.

Tom's success caused me to think very seriously of the wonderful prospects which were possible as a golf professional. Although I had played very little, I knew in my own heart I was quite as good as my brother, and, if he could win such sums of money, there was no reason I should not be able to do so. I did not receive much encouragement from my father in my new ambition to become a professional. My father was himself a golfer, but there had been few opportunities for him to see my play. As a matter of fact, he never did see me play until after I had won my third championship. He had on numerous occasions watched Tom, and always thought he had the makings of a gifted golfer.

As regards myself, he did not think I showed sufficient keenness to excel at the game. Even when I had won a large number of prizes, and had made a reputation for myself, he remained firm to his early convictions. He frequently remarked that although "Harry may win the prizes, it is Tom who plays the golf."

It so happened that Lowe, with whom Tom was working, was requested by Lord Ripon to lay out a nine-hole course on his estate. Tom at once wrote and told me they would want a professional there, and if I decided that such an appointment would suit me, I had better apply for the position right away. This I did, and was engaged.

To return for a moment to the competition among the members of the Working Men's Club to which I have already referred, the conditions of which consisted of six rounds of score play. Only five rounds at this time had been played. Although I was leading by so many strokes that it was almost impossible for anyone to beat me, the sixth and last round was not due to take place for a couple of weeks. It had previously been decided that we should play one round a month. This meant, as I was leaving home, I would not have an opportunity to complete the competition, and, although an assured winner, would not be eligible for the prize. The committee of the club, however, very kindly gave me the necessary permission to play my sixth and last round before leaving for England. That was how I won my first golf tournament.

I BECOME A
PROFESSIONAL

It was in November, 1890, when I was a few months past my twentieth year, that I set out from Jersey on my new career. I recall that my brother Tom met me on my arrival in England. We proceeded to Ripon and I remember as we walked through the town to my lodgings, carrying my golf clubs, the good folks there took us for poachers. A bag of golf clubs in those now distant days was an exceedingly uncommon sight. Today a man walking anywhere with his clubs would attract little or no attention but, at that period, it was a natural mistake for the locals to take us for poachers. For one thing, poaching was certainly more in their minds than golf, if they had even heard of the game, which is doubtful.

I was greenkeeper as well as professional to the Studley Royal Golf Club, in Ripon in Yorkshire. Golf, however, had not taken hold there at this date. In fact so little was played that the summer after my arrival I spent more time at cricket than golf. I remember that I took part in many enjoyable games of cricket while at Ripon. Lord Ripon kept a large staff of gardeners and gamekeepers, and many matches were arranged between different sides, and the rivalry was keen.

The year I spent at Ripon was most enjoyable, and I did not in any way regret having embarked on a new life in what might be called a strange land. I found the gardeners and everyone who worked on the estate good sportsmen. Many an enjoyable evening I spent at the gardeners' "Boffy." This was the sleeping, eating and resting place provided for them, and all kinds of games were indulged in there.

Boxing was very popular with them. I had always been fond of all sports, and was quite willing to try my hand with the gloves. One evening when I arrived at the "Boffy", one of the gardeners called out to me, "Harry, we've got someone who will put you through your paces tonight." My astonishment may be imagined when a fine buxom lass, the daughter of one of the gamekeepers, appeared on the scene, and I was told that she was to be my opponent. The fight did not last very long. This young amazon with a punch that would have done credit to a heavyweight champion landed one fair and square on my nose. As far as I was concerned, that ended any aspirations I may have held of becoming a champion boxer.

Lord Ripon himself did not play golf, but occasionally some of his friends would play a round. There was, however, very little for me to do in the golfing line, and I remember with gratitude the interest of Mr. St. Quintin, who was private secretary to Lord Ripon and a good golfer. On many occasions he put business my way, which, as things were exceedingly quiet in the sales department, was generous to say the least. Mr. St. Quintin would frequently tell me that he would like to try out some clubs. I would select two or three, which I would loan to him, together with a good supply of balls, which he would purchase. There was a lake running through the estate in which eventually nearly all the gutties I had sold him would disappear. Mr. St. Quintin was a fine free hitter of a golf ball, and appeared to thoroughly enjoy having a real good wallop at them. When the supply of balls was exhausted, he would return the clubs. This borrowing of clubs and purchasing of new balls was repeated constantly. He enjoyed himself and at the same time it was indeed an exceedingly nice way of helping a young man along in his new career.

There were occasionally a few good players who played on the links and I had some good games with them. I remember after completing a round with one of them, he told me that I did not get nearly enough golf to give me the slightest chance of improving. The idea that I might ever win a championship had not as yet occurred to me.

I was naturally ambitious. I thought over the advice I had received very seriously and, having chosen to follow the life of a professional golfer, was naturally anxious to secure a position with more opportunities. I had been at Ripon twelve months when I saw an advertisement for a professional at the Bury Golf Club in Lancashire. I decided I would apply for the position, and obtained it.

A curious feature of my going to Bury was that it occurred in the month of November, 1891, exactly twelve months after I had left Jersey to take up my first appointment. The course at Bury was a good nine-hole course. I was again greenkeeper as well as professional. When I say I was greenkeeper and had full charge of the course, I mean this in a literal sense, as there was no one employed to work on the links except myself. It is true that the landlord of the ground on which our course was situated had a fine collection of animals who helped keep the grass down. The mowing and rolling of the greens, and all those things pertaining to the general upkeep of the course, I did myself. It was a rule of the club that I was not to play or teach before four o'clock in the afternoon.

I was getting a good deal more golf than in my previous position, and was beginning to play fairly well. It was only natural that, with more play and keener games with a stiffer class of opponent, I should begin to think seriously about improving my own game. I may say here, and I have often had to make the same statement in days gone by, that I never had a lesson in my life. For one thing, there was no one to teach me, and for another, I had made little effort to seriously improve my golf. I had played more or less as other young golfers would play, just for the fun of the thing. But anything in the nature of attempting to think things out had not, up to this period, occurred to me. However, now it was different.

I may have been fortunate in the fact that, on many occasions, I had plenty of spare time in which to practice. Many people have frequently remarked to me, when they have noticed me either going out or returning from a little

The young Vardon working on his game.

practice with some club or another, "If I could play anything like you, I wouldn't spend my time in practice, I
would be having an enjoyable match." It does not appear
to have occurred to these people that if it had not been for
practice, I should not have been able to play anything
approaching the golf I was able to produce. However
much golf a man may play, it will not, in my firm opinion,
be as valuable as an occasional hour by oneself in a quiet
spot on the links with a club and some balls. The enormous value of practice was readily realized by American
golfers.

Walter J. Travis, who was the first overseas competitor
to gain a victory in the British Amateur Championship,
was a fine example of the benefits of serious practice. It
has been related of him that, when in the course of playing a round he had made a bad stroke, on finishing the
round he would proceed to the exact place where his error
was committed and play the shot over and over again
until he was absolutely satisfied that he had mastered it.

There is not the slightest shadow of doubt that the continued success of the American golfers year after year in
the British Open Championship is the result of time
which they put in regularly in practising their strokes. I
came to the conclusion at Bury that if I was to achieve any
success in the golfing world, I must give some serious
thought to my game. As I was firmly convinced that the
grip which one employs is the first fundamental principle
of a successful game, it was to this point that I first paid
strict attention.

I had, up to this period, always utilized the "palm"
method of gripping my clubs. Those who used this grip,
and it was the one universally employed in these days,
experienced, so it seemed to me, a certain amount of difficulty in controlling the right hand. At impact the right
hand would be apt to overpower the left, thereby causing
a crooked shot.

I do not believe in a master hand or a master arm in connection with the striking of a golf ball. I maintain that as the playing of golf is a two-handed affair, both these members work, or should work, as one. It is absolutely incorrect to assume that the arms, or the wrists, or the hands have to be specially applied when hitting a golf ball. The one important thing that really matters is the club head, and the hands, wrists, and arms should be considered as part of the club, all working together as one piece of machinery. This being the case, I set to work to try out different ways of gripping the club. After trials with many methods, I arrived at the conclusion that the overlapping grip answered the purpose better than any other. It was an easy grip to employ, and it solved to a very appreciable extent the fault of the right hand doing too much work. As I became accustomed to it, I began, when swinging the club, to have the satisfactory feeling that both hands were working as one. There was, I understand, a general impression in the golfing world that I had stated that, unless a player utilized the overlapping grip, he would not be able to aspire to the highest honours in the game. This impression was altogether wrong. I do think—in fact, I will go further and say—I feel sure that except in some rare cases, the overlapping grip is the best one to be employed. So much for the grip. I then began to pay attention to such matters as stance, balance, and many other small but important details which improved my play.

While there has always been different opinions as to whether the square stance or the open stance was the better to use in addressing the ball, I personally have favored the open stance. The chief feature in standing this way is the fact that there is nothing which impedes the club head in coming through first. It appeared to me that it was easier to drive a ball for "carry" with this method of address than with the square stance.

As a final point, the upright swing lends itself more to the open stance than the old-time flatter St. Andrews swing. I had always swung my club in the upright manner, and consequently the open stance was more natural for me.

I made many other experiments in the playing of different strokes, and it was while at Ripon that I learnt the low flying backspin shot with an iron club that is usually known as the push shot. This splendid stroke, in which I became proficient in later years, was to help me secure many noted golfing honours. I have always considered the push shot the master stroke in golf. It is by no means an easy one to learn, but it is well worth all the trouble, patience, and practice which is required if it is to be mastered. Once a player has learnt it, he has realized the full joy of golf. My favourite club for this stroke was the cleek. The stroke actually should never be attempted with anything beyond a three-quarter swing. It is surprising how far and how sure, too, one can hit a half-cleek push shot when the stroke has been mastered.

I must say I thoroughly enjoyed my association with the Bury Golf Club. I had, too, a feeling of great pleasure and pride when I learnt that the club had made me an honorary member. I have on my mantelpiece, as I write, a clock which was sent to me by the members of the club, along with a letter in which they were kind enough to say how much my services to their club had been appreciated.

It was while at Bury that I took part in the first professional match of my life. My opponent was Alexander Herd of Huddersfield. At this period Herd was recognized as a famous player, and so it was only natural that the outcome of the match was looked upon as a foregone conclusion. The arrangement was that we should play thirty-six holes, home and home. The first thirty-six took place at Herd's course at Huddersfield, and although I cannot recall exactly how many holes he was up at the finish, I do know I had lost too many to have any chance of beating him. I had hoped to do better at Bury, but I didn't. Although I was disappointed at the outcome of my first professional match, there was some consolation in the fact that I was completely cured of my early complaint of nervousness.

BREAKING THROUGH
IN THE
1896 BRITISH OPEN

In 1893 I decided to enter for the Open Championship, which was being played at Prestwick. Before the big event took place, I took part in my first professional competition, which was held at Kilmacolm in Scotland. The tournament consisted of thirty-six holes, medal play. All things considered, I did quite well, tying with Hugh Kirkaldy for second place. Kirkaldy wanted to settle matters in a playoff, but my brother Tom strongly advised me not to do so, as I was as yet very inexperienced, and he thought that I had done well enough as a start. Willie Fernie, who for many years was professional at Troon, was the winner. Fernie was very popular. He was a fine putter, and had a beautiful swing with his full shots. He played most of his wooden-club strokes with a hook, as so many of the old Scotch players did at that period. This type of driving, could, on occasions, cause a considerable amount of trouble. Fernie, however, was a perfect master of the controlled "hook".

In the championship, I was drawn with Willie Campbell. Although rather overawed by his reputation, I started out well. Unfortunately, I was unable to keep it up and broke down rather badly in the later stages. However, I finished ahead of Campbell and, under the circumstances, did as well as I could have been expected to. Willie Campbell, at this date, was possibly a little past his best, and could not quite reproduce the strokes of which, in his prime, he had been such a master. Although inclined to be short off the tee and through the green, Willie still had an extremely accurate short game.

J.H. Taylor, with whom in later years I was to have so many splendid battles, also made his first appearance in this championship. I recall that in the first round he scored a 75, which with the gutty ball at Prestwick was a fine showing. His play was so accurate, it was said that his chief hazards were the guide flags. Willie Auchterlonie was the winner. He was an able all-round golfer. His victory made a great deal of difference to him, and he settled down to the business of club making and, for a time, his clubs were all the rage. Auchterlonie attended entirely to his business and never took part in any of the big tournaments afterwards.

The first big success I achieved was a competition which took place at Portrush in Ireland. Nearly all the big professionals of the day were present. There was a selling-sweep on the tournament. A syndicate bought most of the players, and I remember I was sold for a shilling.

The tournament was due to be decided by match play and, as I was drawn against Andrew Kirkaldy in the first round, Jack White, with whom I was staying, told me he would like to introduce me to my opponent. It happened that as we were walking in the street we met Kirkaldy, and the introduction having taken place, Andrew, after looking me up and down said, "Youngster, what the hell do you want to come all this way for, you've no earthly chance?" (*Earthly* was not exactly the word he used.) Blunt and abrupt he may have been outwardly, but underneath he was a fine fellow. The following day a heavy wind was blowing, and at the first hole I had a putt of not more than a yard to secure the lead. Every moment the ball threatened to roll over and I waited for it to steady itself. To hole this putt meant a good deal to me. I felt a good start was everything. The waiting appeared to exasperate Andrew, and he explained, "Man, d'ye ken I'm caul, are ye gaun to keep me waiting her a'nicht?" Playing the putt quickly, I missed it, and the hole was halved. I determined after this to set about my opponent, and by the time we reached the turn had secured a comfortable lead. At this point, two of the holes ran parallel to each other, and Andrew's brother Hugh and his partner were going to one as we were going to the other. Hugh asked Andrew the state of the game, and on being informed that I was five up, muttered in tones of distress, "Ma conscience," as he passed along.

In the final Sandy Herd defeated me on the last green after a good match, and so I had to be satisfied with the prize for the runner-up. I may add that I never received anything out of the selling sweep from the syndicate!

Sandwich was the venue of the Open Championship in 1894. I did better than in the previous year, finishing fifth. My scores of 80 and 81 were among the lowest combined returns on the second day. J.H. Taylor was the winner that year with an aggregate of 326 for the 72 holes. I have always considered Sandwich the finest test of golf in the world.

The championship the following year, 1895, took place at St. Andrews, and J.H. Taylor was again the winner. I brought in the lowest score in the first round, but could only tie for ninth place at the finish. Sandy Herd was always considered rather unfortunate not to win this championship. In the last round he was forced to play through a severe thunderstorm. When it was Taylor's time to start on his final eighteen holes, the storm had cleared, and the condition of the course gave him every opportunity to bring into force the mashie pitches for which he was already famous. He took advantage of his opportunities. For some reason or other, I have never been very fond of St. Andrews. There are, of course, many excellent holes, but somehow it has never really appealed to me. As most golfers probably know, the St. Andrews player nearly always plays his run-up approaches, long or short, with a wooden putter.

Early in the year of 1896, I left Bury. Once again it was through my brother Tom that I secured the job of professional at Ganton in Yorkshire. He told me it was a superior course and that it would be a good position for me. I found Ganton, although inland, to be a true seaside links. There were eighteen holes, and the turf was excellent. Most of the members lived in the big cities of Sheffield, Bradford, and Leeds, and came to Ganton to play in

Vardon's first big success: runner-up to Sandy Herd in the first Irish Professional Golf Tournament held at Royal Portrush in 1895. Vardon, left, watches Herd putting on the eighteenth green in the final round. Herd won 1 up.

the Spring, Summer and Autumn meetings. They usually managed to arrange to take a week's holiday about the time these competitions were held.

Soon after taking up my duties at Ganton, a match was arranged for me against J.H. Taylor. This was indeed a great test as J.H. had won the Open Championship the two previous years. I was playing well and was not over-awed by his reputation. I looked upon it in the light that I had nothing to lose and everything to gain. The match was decided over thirty-six holes, and I remember playing outstanding golf, gaining an easy victory by eight and six.

Several of the famous Yorkshire cricketers used to play on our links. Long John Tunnicliffe and Wildred Rhodes, the famous slow left-handed bowler, were two that I re-call. Rhodes frequently played during the Scarborough festival. He was a good golfer but not as good as Tunni-cliffe, whom I had known at Bury, where he had a sport-ing goods shop.

I remember that David Hunter, the well-known York-shire wicket-keeper, did not think golf difficult and bet Tunnicliffe that he could step up to the tee and hit a good drive. Tunnicliffe told him he would not hit the ball at all. Hunter, to his great surprise, missed the ball completely many times. He could not understand why it was that a man, who had his eye trained for hitting a cricket ball, was unable to hit a teed up stationary object. It is just the fact that the object at golf is stationary that makes it more difficult to strike than the moving ball of such games as cricket and tennis. I did not play much cricket at this period, but took an interest in football and was instru-mental in starting the Ganton Football Club.

I had four assistants working for me in my shop at Ganton. There was very little golf played on the week-ends after the winter had set in, and as football was ex-tremely popular in Ganton and the surrounding villages, I decided it would be an excellent idea to have a team of

The first of the Great Triumvirate to win the British Open, J.H. Taylor, holes the winning putt in the 1895 Open at St. Andrews for his second consecutive title. The previous year he won at Sandwich.

our own. The village of Sherburn already had a good side, and my proposal was welcomed with enthusiasm. Our team was soon completed. There were many young lads who were exceedingly anxious to play. We had a very good team, too. A young lad named Clarkson, who played inside right, was a fine footballer, and Fred Beck, one of the Jersey family of that name, also played for us. Beck was a professional golfer at Filey and proved himself to be a very fast and tricky wing forward. I played centre forward and was appointed captain. No gate money was charged, collections were made by a house to house visit of the local golfers, and, in any case, we were never in debt.

Every Saturday afternoon, throughout the winter months, we had a match against one of the local villages. The big game of the year was the one against the village of Sherburn. This match took place on Christmas Day, and was always a keen battle. The rivalry between the two village teams was sharp, and no quarter was asked for or given. On the whole, I can say that we were able to give our supporters good value for their money. I played for the Ganton team for several seasons. On my return from my American golf tour in the fall of 1900, I continued to play for them, acting as goalie.

I was looking forward to the Open Championship of '96, which was to take place at Muirfield. The success I had achieved in my match against Taylor, a few weeks before the Open was due to start, had given me a good deal of encouragement.

At this time we played thirty-six holes each of the two days of the Open. At the end of the first day's play, I was well up with the leaders, Taylor occupying the place just above me.

On the second day it so happened that J.H. was playing a few holes ahead of me. Late in the contest it became apparent that the issue would be decided between us.

The Ganton football team, Vardon in front row, fourth from left.

Three or four holes from the finish I was told how many
strokes I had to take to win. When I arrived on the last tee,
I was set with an extremely difficult problem. I needed a
four to gain a victory outright and a five to tie, which
would give me the right to play off with Taylor for the
championship. The last hole at Muirfield was a testing
one, requiring a good drive and an exceptional brassie to
reach the green. There was, however, a perilous bunker
guarding the green, and while there was little difficulty in
securing the necessary five which would enable me to tie,
I might very easily take a six in my attempt to reach the
green with my second shot. After hitting a good tee shot
the temptation to have a "go" for the green with my
brassie was very strong. The thought flashed through my
brain that if I were successful in carrying the hazard and
placing my ball on the green, I would, in the space of a
very few minutes, have gained the coveted honour of
champion. On the other hand, if the second shot was not
almost perfectly played, I should find myself in this formidable hazard and might very easily require a six for the
hole, thus losing any chance of a tie. This was the problem
that confronted me.

A championship hung upon the decision. I admit I
hesitated. I think I might have elected to take my iron
and play the safe game in any case. Thoughts flash
through the brain with lightning rapidity during such a
moment, and to me this was an occasion of staggering
importance.

The final decision, however, was the result of allowing
my eyes to wander among the spectators in front of me. I
caught sight of my friend, James Kay, of Seaton Carew,
making frantic efforts to attract my attention. He was
pointing with his hand to the ground this side of the
bunker, and there could be no question that he was giving
me his advice to play short. To me the problem was
solved, and I was determined I would play short. This I

did, and, holing out in five, tied with Taylor for the championship with an aggregate of 316 for the seventy-two holes.

The last round of the championship was concluded on a Thursday, and another tournament had been arranged at North Berwick for the following day. We were given permission to take part in this event, which would enable us to play our tie off in the championship on the Saturday. When we teed up again at Muirfield, I was feeling extremely fit and well, and had the feeling that I was going to achieve the ambition of all golfers—winning the Open Championship. It is possible that another reason for this feeling of confidence was the fact that I had already beaten Taylor once. I started out in a way that certainly justified my confidence—after the first six holes, I held a lead of five strokes. My opponent soon settled down and, playing some brilliant golf, reduced my lead to a single stroke. At the end of the first eighteen holes, however, I was two shots to the good.

When we set out for the second eighteen, I lost my lead with the very first stroke I made. The first hole at Muirfield was a one-shotter with a wood running along the left hand side of the course. Taking my driving-iron, I pulled the ball into the wood, which was out of bounds, and, as the penalty at that time was a loss of stroke and distance, I had to tee up again and play three. I made no mistake on this occasion, and secured a five, but Taylor obtained his par three, and my precious lead disappeared. My brother Tom, who was carrying my clubs, saw my disappointment and encouraged me with the words, "Never mind, Harry, you'll soon get those two back again."

During the next three holes, I managed to gain a shot at every one of them. Try as my opponent would, he was not able to make up this deficit, although he had reduced my lead to two when we had holed out on the sixteenth green. I was now two strokes to the good with two holes to be played, a position which seemed to assure me the championship. I was to make my position still more secure at the following hole by sinking a long putt across the green for a three. Tom took great pains to point out the line to me. After studying the putt for myself, I told him I thought it would be better if I took a different line. This I did and the ball dropped into the hole. My feelings as I stood on the eighteenth tee may readily be imagined. On that tee two days previously, I had been faced with as difficult a situation as possibly any golfer has ever been called upon to face. Now things were entirely altered.

From my point of view, there was no problem. All I had to do was to play for a safe five. Taylor, too, had little difficulty in choosing his course of action. His only chance was to reach the green with his second shot and secure a three, in the hope that I might drop a stroke somewhere or other and take a six. As things turned out I had a five without any difficulty, and it was my opponent who required the six. Taylor's gallant bid for a three met with the unhappy fate which I had feared might befall me two days previously. Although playing a fine brassie shot, he was caught in the bunker guarding the green, and any hope he may have had of retaining his championship was lost. I have frequently been asked my feelings when the last putt had been holed on the home green. I can only say the obvious—it was an occasion I will never forget as long as I live. To achieve the greatest ambition a golfer can aspire to prevents anyone having any clear, distinct thoughts. This is how it seemed to me. With the cheering going on all around me, and with everyone talking at the same time, I was too stunned to have any more feelings than those. I would not be telling the truth if I related how overjoyed I felt at that moment. As it is my wish to tell my readers the exact truth, I can only say that I was dazed and unable to speak.

I stood on the eighteenth green a long time as if my feet

had taken root there. A little later on, I realized I had really won the championship.

Another question which has often been asked me is which was my favourite club at this date. I have always been very fond of my driver. A few years later I might have answered this question by selecting my brassie. At this period, however, my driving iron was my favourite. When distance was required, I was able to obtain a very long ball with it and could hit it so far that Andrew Kirkaldy used to call it my iron driver. My favourite shot with it was the push shot, played with either a half or three-quarter swing according to the distance required. To play this stroke correctly, a golfer should never employ anything more than a three-quarter swing. I have always looked upon Muirfield as a good test of golf, and was unable to agree with the remark of Andrew Kirkaldy that it was just an "ould Watter Medie." In those days it was more of an inland than a seaside links, but with the gutty ball it was a real test of the game. In later years the links were extended beyond the wall, which at this period used to surround it, into the sand hills. This alteration has given it more of a seaside appearance.

Before leaving the scene of this, my first victory in the Open Championship, I should say something about my putting. I had played extremely well in the seventy-two holes of the championship, but my putting had not been nearly as good as the rest of my game. However, in the playoff I never putted better in my life. I holed many long putts, and so close were my approach putts to the tin that very little actual holing-out was required. I feel sure the remarkable change in such a short space of time was the result of a visit to Ben Sayers' shop on the day on which I was competing in the North Berwick Tournament before the playoff in the championship. I mentioned to the club maker that, as I was not satisfied with my putting, I wanted to obtain a new putter. I had been playing with one of the bent-necked variety and decided I might do better with a change.

While looking round the shop I saw an old cleek in the corner which appeared as if it had been thrown away and discarded forever. On picking it up, I found it to be a very light club—too light for the task for which it had been designed. The idea suddenly occurred to me that if the old shaft was taken out and a new short one put in, it would make a top-notch putter. As soon as this was done, I took my new purchase in my hands. I felt sure I had acquired exactly what I had been looking for. It was to this old, discarded cleek that I owed the remarkable improvement in my putting on the following day, and, in a sense, the championship.

MY HISTORIC MATCH
WITH WILLIE PARK

In 1897 the Open Championship was held at Hoylake and resulted in a victory for H. H. Hilton on what was his home course. Those critics who have put forward the claim that Harold Hilton was the greatest British amateur golfer have sound support for this contention, and I agree with them. When it is remembered that he won the Open Championship on two occasions and carried off four victories in the Amateur Championship, it is difficult to see how any other amateur player could be put forward as superior or even equal to him. Although he proved himself to be a good match player, it was generally conceded that he was better at medal play. Hilton was in every way a sound golfer, relying on accuracy rather than the wild swiping which appears to be somewhat prevalent amongst the first-class players of the present time. He was never a long hitter, but he understood the art of placing his shots, an art which today does not appear to reach the standard of the old days. His control and accuracy with his spoon was astounding. I consider Harold Hilton and George Duncan the finest exponents of this club I have ever seen. Another fine player with the spoon was my old friend Sandy Herd, and it was a club which I myself used with considerable success at one period.

No discussion of famous amateur golfers would be complete without a reference to John Ball. There is no doubt that he must rank very high. One has only to recall his wonderful feat of winning eight Amateur Championships, which is a record in the world of golf. Johnny Ball was also the first amateur to win the Open and Amateur Championships in the same year—a record which stood for over thirty years and one that has never been equalled by a British-born player. It was in 1890 that he gained these two victories, and yet twenty-two years later we find him once again the champion. He was one of the few famous players, Sandy Herd being another, who retained the old "palm" grip throughout their golfing life. Johnny

Ball was obviously adept in all departments of the game. His outstanding club was the cleek, which so many players have found extremely difficult. Ball, however, was a master with the cleek and was able to play many different types of shots with it. I should add that he was very popular with his fellow golfers and considered a model sportsman.

In the championship of 1897, won by Harold Hilton, I did not do well. Jimmie Braid, who was rapidly making a reputation for himself, finished second—one stroke behind the winner. There was an exciting finish to the championship the following year when it was played at Prestwick. In the last round, the struggle for supremacy was narrowed down to a contest between Willie Park and myself. At the end of the third round Willie was three strokes ahead of me, a lead which appeared to be insurmountable. In the final round I was playing a hole in front of Park, and we were naturally watching each other very closely the whole way. I played excellent golf to the turn and wiped out my deficit of three strokes. Thus I was able to set out on the return journey playing my opponent on level terms. I finished steadily, and then stood amongst the huge crowd which surrounded the home green to see this famous Scotch player finish. He had to get a three at the eighteenth hole, Clock, to tie with me. His drive was a good one and finished on the corner of the green, and, as he was renowned for his putting, it seemed as though once again I was to be involved in a playoff for the Open Championship. Park's long putt stopped about a yard from the hole, which to my way of thinking was much too close. As the crowd pressed round the green to see him play his short putt, it so happened that I was elbowed out. I stood at the edge of the crowd unable to see anything at all. Never in the whole course of my playing career have I felt so uncomfortable and nervous as I did during those two or three minutes. At last, after what seemed an eternity, there rose from all round the ring a disappointed O-o-oh! I made no attempt to look at his ball which was, of course, still outside the hole, for the crowd had told me in plain words that I had won the championship for the second time. Willie Park was playing brilliantly at this period, and it was only because I played as well as I ever did in my life that I was able to defeat him.

One of the most important events in my career and the greatest match I ever played was my contest with Willie Park. Park, who was unhappy at having lost the championship at Prestwick by a putt, challenged me to a thirty-six-hole, home-and-home match for £100 a side. Park named Musselburgh and Ganton as the two courses where he wished the match to be played. While I was willing to accept his challenge to play a seventy-two-hole match over two courses, I would not agree to Mussel-burgh as one of them. I told him that I was quite willing for the match to be decided at North Berwick and Ganton. As North Berwick was as much his home course as Mus-selburgh, I saw no reason why he should object. I felt sure that Musselburgh was not a suitable type of links on which to hold a contest of this kind. On account of the publicity regarding the match, it was only natural to ex-pect that there would be an exceedingly large number of spectators to witness the event. Owing to the fact that Musselburgh was a nine-hole course and a small one at that, I was firmly convinced that it would be better not to play there.

Eventually we agreed to hold the encounter over the North Berwick and Ganton courses with North Berwick being the first venue. While this controversy was going on, the season was passing, and it was not until the fol-lowing year that all arrangements were completed.

I was playing very fine golf in the spring of 1899. The game seemed easy to me. I felt as if I could step up to the ball with any club and hit it exactly where I wanted to without any effort. My accuracy with both wood and iron was almost uncanny. My driving was long and accurate, and I could judge my shots up to the hole with my iron clubs so correctly that almost always the ball would end up within a few yards of the flagstick.

I had with diligent practice become highly proficient with my brassie, and it was principally by the aid of the testing shots up to the hole with this club that I gained my third Open victory in the 1899 championship. At the end of the first day's play, I led the field with a score of 152. Taylor was second a stroke behind, and Jimmie Braid and Willie Park were third with 156.

The second day proved to be a very difficult one, for a strong wind was blowing and Sandwich, especially in the age of the gutty ball, was a severe test even in calm weather. I played well and my brassie shots continued to be exceptionally good. I frequently laid the ball dead near the hole, and in the end scored an easy win. Jack White finished second to me in this championship.

Soon after the championship, my big match with Willie Park took place. There was an unbelievably large crowd of spectators at North Berwick for the opening round. In fact, it was one of the biggest golf crowds that I have ever played before in my life. All golfing Scotland appeared to have turned out. I would say there were fully ten thousand people on the links, and if it had not been that the Prince of Wales was visiting Edinburgh that day, there probably would have been several thousand more. Large as this crowd was, it was perfectly managed, and never in any way interfered with the play of a single stroke. The arrangements in every way were admirable. As it was impossible for a large section of the crowd to see the game, two flags were made, one white with a red "P" on it, the other red with a white "V" on it. When Park won a hole the flag with his initial was hoisted, and the "V" flag was sent up when I won a hole. When a half was recorded both flags were waved. Thus it was possible for everyone to know the result of each hole.

At each teeing ground there was a rope three hundred yards in length down the fairway, which was controlled by fourteen policemen, and numerous honorary officials. C.C. Broadwood, who was the captain of the Ganton Club, acted as my referee, and F.G. Tait served in the same capacity for Park. Norman and Mansfield Hunter were the fore caddies. I had played well on my two practice rounds—I had two 76s—and on the day we teed up I was ready.

Willie Park's caddie, "Fiery", was a notable character, one of the old type Scotch caddies who took a real interest in their masters. Nearly all the old Scotch caddies carried the clubs of their employer under their arm, and "Fiery" was no exception, although he took a bag with him in case of rain. "Fiery" knew as much, if not more, about the play of his famous master as his master did and always handed him the correct club before he asked for it.

My brother Tom caddied for me as he had at Muirfield in the 1896 Open. While on the subject of famous caddies, I recall an incident which occurred the evening before the beginning of the match. I was taking a walk with my brother when Big Crawford, possibly the most famous of all the North Berwick caddies, suddenly appeared round a corner. As he saw us, he threw a big horseshoe at me, which nearly brained my brother. He explained that he was tossing the horseshoe over my head for luck; he had backed me to win with every penny he possessed. His idea of bringing me luck might very easily have had a very different ending from that which he intended, but it was impossible to be annoyed when he explained the situation. Big Crawford was a great character and many tales have been published about him. Actually we had two caddies each, although these understudies did not take any part in the proceedings. They were two friends who wished to be sure of obtaining a view of the match. Each carried a spare set of clubs, one for my opponent and one for myself. This enabled them to see perfectly.

Play opened in ideal weather, and with the sun shining brilliantly we stepped on the tee of the famous Point Garry Out hole. As the challenger, Park drove the first ball, and a great event of my golfing life had commenced. On the outward half the game was so even that the first nine holes were all halved, each of us reaching the turn in thirty-eight strokes. Although I was more accurate in the long game than my opponent, he splendidly upheld the reputation which he had earned for himself as a magnificent putter. Time after time, when I appeared certain to gain the lead, his splendid holing out saved him. There was yet another half at the tenth. At the eleventh, Quarry In, a curious incident happened. Park, of course, still had the honour and drove a fine ball straight up the centre of the fairway. I drove, and my ball pitched right on top of his, knocking it forward. We were unable to see this peculiar incident from the tee, but were informed about it by the fore caddies. My opponent's ball was replaced in its original position. I found my ball in a very heavy lie and eventually lost the hole. Thus Park had the satisfaction of drawing first blood.

After the Quarry In, the match became all even again at the thirteenth, named The Pit. It has always been the custom on Scotch courses to name each hole on the links. Perfection, the fourteenth, was halved in good fours, and by winning the Redan with a par three, I gained the lead for the first time. The following hole was halved which left me one up and two to play on the first round. At the seventeenth, Point Garry In, Park played one of the finest strokes which I have ever seen. His third shot ran over the green and onto the beach, and, as I was comfortably on the green in three, it looked as if I was certain to add another hole to my lead. When Park came up to his ball, he found it in such a position that he was forced to play a left-handed shot, which gave me further reason to anticipate winning the hole. However, my opponent played a magnificent stroke onto the green and holed his putt for a five, while I required three putts for a six. Thus I lost a hole which I had looked upon as a certain win. The position of the game was once more all even, and with my opponent securing the home hole he had the advantage of a single point at lunch.

The crowd had increased in numbers when we set out for the afternoon round. So keen and close had the match proved to be in the morning that a terrific struggle was expected. Although there was nothing approaching the sensational sequence of halves which had occurred on the outward half of the first round, the play was full of drama, and the enthusiasm of the spectators was intense. As a matter of fact, it was not until the fourth that a halved hole was recorded. By winning the first I once again drew level with my opponent. Park took the lead at the second but, with a four to his six at the following hole, I again squared the match. There followed a run of five halved holes. At the ninth, however, with a four to Park's five, I forged ahead, and with another win at the tenth became two holes up on the Scotsman. Park at this stage proved beyond any shadow of doubt what a fine match player he was. Just when I thought I was in a secure position, he promptly dashed my hopes of piling up a commanding lead by winning the next two holes. And so the contest was all even once again. It had been a great battle, and the huge gallery had witnessed many fluctuations. As if to prove that I too was a good match player, I followed up the loss of these two holes by winning the fifteenth, Redan, and sixteenth, Gate, to regain my advantage of two. Point Garry In was halved, and at the eighteenth, Home, I had a splendid opportunity to increase my lead to three,

North Berwick: the end of the day's play.

my putt for a win stopping on the very lip of the hole. A half in four was the result, and at the close of a memorable day's play with the crowd cheering heartily, I was leading by two holes.

The quality of our golf was extremely good. I was driving far and straight. Park, although occasionally wild with his wooden club shots, was approaching and putting extremely well. I cannot say that I was altogether satisfied with my putting as I missed several short putts which I should have holed. However, to have gained a lead of two holes on Park's home course was good enough.

On Thursday morning, July 20th, Park and I set out to play the final 36 holes of our match at my home course,

Ganton: Park putting but Vardon in charge.

Ganton. Since my return from North Berwick I had continued to play well, and it was with a feeling of the utmost
confidence that I viewed the forthcoming encounter. My
readers must not be led to imagine by these remarks that
I, in any way, underestimated the ability of my opponent.
He had given sufficient proof of his golfing and match-
playing qualities at North Berwick. My feelings of confidence were based on totally different lines. For one thing,
I felt that my work on the greens at North Berwick had not
been as good as I hoped. I was satisfied that I was able to
outplay my opponent in the long game, and I fully expected to gain an even further advantage in this department. At Ganton, especially from the back tees, it was
necessary to hit the ball for "carry." This was my natural

Many of Willie Park's drives were snared by the long carries from the tee at Ganton. Above, the carry from the eighteenth tee.

method with my wooden clubs. Park, however, played, as was the custom with nearly all the old type of Scotch golfers, a low ball with a "draw." When this hook was under full control, it enabled the player to obtain fine distance, which to an enormous extent was the outcome of the run obtained from a right-to-left shot. The player who adopted this method of driving, where long carries were necessary, was at a distinct disadvantage. The first three holes at Ganton demanded long carries from the back tees, and for this reason, unless Park did not try to draw his drives, I felt that I should win all three of these holes.

In addition, I felt sure I would give a better account of myself on the greens at Ganton than I had at North Berwick. The final reason for my confidence was that Park, in his practice rounds, had not exhibited his best form.

My prediction regarding the first three holes turned out to be correct. I won all three. Park failed, as I had thought might be the case, to carry the hazards from the tee with his drives. Thus early on I had practically made the outcome of the match secure. I really did play good golf that day at Ganton. I was hitting a long accurate ball from the teeing ground, and my shots to the hole were on target. My putting, too, was much better than it had been at North Berwick, and I can truthfully say that I have never in the course of my career played sounder all-round golf. My victory, which I eventually secured by the margin of eleven up and ten to play, was possibly made easier for me because of my opponent's inability to play his best golf.

1900: MY FIRST AMERICAN TOUR

Toward the end of 1899, A.G. Spalding made me an offer for an extended tour in the United States. They would give me a fixed sum for every exhibition match in which I took part and, of course, pay all my expenses.

I was quite willing to undertake the tour. During the past two years I could say, without any boasting, that I had proved myself to be the leading golfer in this country. I knew, too, that at this period I was at my very best, and felt sure that in my exhibitions I would be able to give a good account of myself. The idea of a trip to the United States appealed to me very strongly. I was anxious to see this great country, and apart from the financial benefit which I should derive from the tour, fully expected to enjoy the novel experience of visiting a new land. Although I made up my mind to accept the offer, I came to the conclusion that, instead of receiving a sum for each match, I would rather receive a lump sum to cover all my engagements. Spalding was quite willing to agree to this arrangement. There is no doubt I should have made more money by their original offer, but I felt I would rather be paid a fixed price and be free of any further financial worry. Everything having been satisfactorily settled, and the necessary permission having been given me by the committee of my club, it was decided I should make a start early in the following year. I left these shores on January 27th, 1900, in the American liner St. Paul and landed in America on February 3rd, and was met by my manager, Charles S. Cox, who took me to the Broadway Central Hotel. I recall, very vividly, that I was soon in the midst of the newspaper reporters. This was an experience which I am not likely to forget. Anyone who has been interviewed by an American newspaperman will realize how extremely careful he must be when discussing anything with them. They are good fellows, and I personally never had any reason to complain of unjust criticism. They have, however, exceptionally imaginative minds

Vardon, on left, with Alex Finlay at Palm Beach.

and can create several columns for their papers out of a few questions and answers. The American golf reporters knew very little about the game of golf, but they made up for their lack of knowledge by their wonderful imaginations. It was amusing and a little alarming to open the morning newspaper and find huge headlines commenting on my arrival and giving accounts of exclusive interviews I had given. Maybe, in the excitement of arriving in a strange country, I did not remember everything I had said. However, if I said as much as they printed, I must have done a great deal of talking.

My first match took place at Lawrence Harbour, New Jersey, on February 12th. Lawrence Harbour Country Club was a nine-hole course. The weather for this first match was terrible. I remember that the clay greens were unplayable and that temporary ones had to be used. Notwithstanding these difficulties, I lowered the course record and defeated my two opponents, whose best ball I played, nine up and eight to play over thirty-six holes.

After this auspicious start, I journeyed to Florida, and at the St. Augustine Club met Willie Smith, the holder of the American championship, in a thirty-six hole contest. Willie was one of several brothers who learned the game at Carnoustie in Scotland. He was a fine player. The large gathering of spectators expected to witness a close match and, as events turned out, this proved to be the case. I was able to defeat Willie two up with one to play after a rousing contest.

I played a good many exhibition matches in the south, the most notable of which were against Alex Finlay, who I defeated at Palm Beach one up, and George Low, who I dominated six up and five to play in Miami. I lost a match at Ormonde against Bernard Nicholls, the only man to defeat me single-handed throughout my tour. There was no grass on the links at Ormonde Beach, and it was a difficult proposition after having been used to playing from turf. Anything in the nature of a pitch shot was absolutely impossible there, and it was necessary to play a run-up shot for approaches of all lengths. Ormonde Beach was, at this period, an up-and-coming resort. There was a fine stretch of sand which was utilized by visitors for cycling. By attaching sails to their bicycles, they were able to travel with the wind for many miles along the vast stretch of sand. One other thing: I have never seen such a collection of magnificent wild birds in my life.

Another match I played in which I struck the ball particularly well was against Willie Dunn and took place in Scarsdale, New York. My score of seventy-three in the first round of this thirty-six hole match was a record for the course. I went on to defeat Dunn by the large margin of fifteen up and fourteen to play. Another round which gave me great satisfaction was against Alex Finlay at Pittsburgh. I completed the first eighteen holes in sixty-nine, and won the match twelve and eleven.

When I look back on this tour, I realize that I was, to some extent, responsible for the great golf craze in America. A crowd of spectators numbering between one or two thousand was quite a common occurrence at my exhibitions. The crowds had little practical knowledge of golf, but they were well behaved and courteous. They were scrupulously fair to me and sometimes ignored the match and concentrated only on my strokes. For the last two years the game had seemed very easy to me and I could hit the ball well with every club in my bag. In the dry American climate, I was able to drive the gutty ball farther than I had ever done before.

The Americans seemed to appreciate the way I hit my tee shots for carry. When they saw the ball driven high in this manner, it appealed to them as resembling a home run in their national sport, baseball. Their interest in how the different strokes were executed was quickly aroused, and it was almost laughable to hear the many heated ar-

Vardon returned to Britain to defend his Open title at St. Andrews in 1900. Here he is pictured driving off the first tee with Old Tom Morris, left, and Sandy Herd, right, watching.

guments about how I achieved my results. The Americans quickly grasped any particular point which they thought was an important part of the swing, and no technical detail however small appeared to escape them. This kind of interest in the mechanics of the golf swing was new to me.

After three months in the States, I returned home to defend my title in the 1900 Open at St. Andrews. I was particularly keen to win this championship and make it three in a row. However, it was with more of a feeling of hope than assurance that I viewed the forthcoming event. After several months of play on courses where it had been necessary to adopt different methods from those which one employed at home, coupled with the fact that I had been engaged in strenuous play the whole time I had been away, I would have a hard time being at my best. There

By defeating J. H. Taylor in the open golf championship of America he won the title, champion of the world.

Vardon after winning the 1900 American Open at the Chicago Golf Club.

was also the sudden change in climatic conditions to be taken into consideration.

All in all, my fears proved to be well-founded. J.H. Taylor, who was in magnificent form, proved to be the winner, and I finished in second place.

Soon after the championship, I returned to the United States and continued my tour. I played exhibition matches in different parts of the country, appearing in many games in New York state and the New England states. I also journeyed into Canada, where I enjoyed some delightful golf.

I was keen to win the 1900 American Open Championship on the fine course of the Chicago Golf Club in Wheaton, Illinois. I thought it would be a fitting climax to the successful tour I had had so far. There was another reason I was eager to win: J.H. Taylor, who had beaten me at St. Andrews in the British Open, had come over from England to take part in the American championship. From my point of view, the fact that Taylor was to compete added special interest to the competition. I was anxious to have my revenge.

Willie Smith, who was the holder of the title, George Low, and all the leading American players were also competing. As was only natural, especially with the presence of Taylor and myself, Willie Smith was determined to score another victory. A success in the championship would have been fitting compensation for the victories I had already gained over him. Taylor also was bent on winning, as he would then be the holder of both the British and American Championships in the same year. Thus an exciting contest was anticipated. As things turned out, however, the outcome depended on the struggle between J.H. and myself. The championship took place in beautiful weather, and a large and fashionable crowd followed the players. President Thomas of the United States Golf Association said afterwards that it was the biggest crowd ever seen at a golf event in America. Although the gallery was very enthusiastic, they were extremely well controlled and did not interfere with the players.

At the end of the first day's play I led the field with a total of 157 for the 36 holes. Taylor was second, one stroke behind. J.H. had a fine 76 in the opening round, but required six strokes more in the afternoon. I was playing very steady golf all day, as my scores of 79 and 78 indicated. Of the American players, Dave Bell, who was attached to the Midlothian Club, did best with an aggregate of 162. George Low, who was professional at Dyker Meadow, had 164, and Willie Smith was one stroke further behind. In the third round I came in with a 76 to Taylor's 79 and led the field by four shots. Dave Bell who had 83, and Willie Smith with 80 were tied for third place, nine strokes behind my leading total. Thus, with eighteen holes to be played, I found myself in an almost invulnerable position. It was only necessary to play steadily in my last round to win the championship. I finished with a final round of 80 for a four-round total of 313. J.H. was second with 315. Dave Bell with a total of 323 was the leading American player, and Lawrence Auchterlonie of Glen View occupied fourth position with a score of 327. Willie Smith was next with 328. I was thrilled to have won the American Open Championship, and the reception I received at the conclusion of the big event could not, in any way, have been more sincere if the victory had been gained by an American.

I had covered roughly 100,000 miles since I first left England almost a year earlier. I had played in innumerable exhibition matches to enthusiastic crowds, producing the finest golf of my life. The tour was a success beyond my wildest dreams. As I sailed home on the "Majestic", I was exhausted but exhilarated.

THE RUBBER-CORED BALL, ANOTHER OPEN VICTORY, AND ILLNESS

Late in the month of December, 1900, I arrived back in England. After my long tour and the many matches in which I had engaged, I needed a rest from competitive golf. On my arrival at Ganton I was pleased to hear that the football club, which I had started some years previously, was having a successful season. I think I am right in saying they had not lost a match. It was with a feeling of much pleasure that I again accepted the captaincy of the club. I did not feel as if I was competent to continue to play centre-forward for them, but I readily agreed to act as goalkeeper. We had a wonderful season.

The 1901 Open Championship was held at Muirfield, where I had won my first Open five years before. I was eager to win again, and at the end of the first day's play, I felt I was in a good position to do so. James Braid and I led the field with a score of 155 for the thirty-six holes. Our nearest rival was J.H. Taylor, seven strokes back. In the third round Braid came in with a splendid 74 and, as I required a 79, he secured an advantage of five strokes. Taylor with a fine 74 had improved his position and was now only two shots behind me. In the concluding round, I managed to gain three strokes on Braid but that was not good enough. He won by three shots with a total of 309. As in the previous year, I was runner-up.

Braid's success—his first in the Open—was by no means unexpected. He had displayed increasingly good form during the past few years. I had seen enough of his play to realize it was only a question of time before J.H. and I would have a serious rival to contend with. He was an unusually powerful player, capable of hitting the gutty ball tremendous distances. His powers of recovery, too, were exceptional. His was a popular victory, and deservedly so: he was one of the best fellows in golf.

The year 1902 ushered in a revolution in the game of golf. A new type of ball made its appearance on the links.

It is not too much to say that the Haskell, the first rubber-cored ball, changed the game. When the new ball was firmly established, golf underwent such drastic changes that to those of us who were brought up with the gutty, it became almost unrecognizable. This change was not immediate. When the possibilities were realized, however, the old solid ball was doomed forever. I personally shall always regret the passing of the gutty. I am firmly convinced that with its passing much of the real skill of golf was gone forever.

Let us take the case of wooden-club play. In the days of the solid ball it was necessary for the drives to be properly struck if anything approaching a good round was to be recorded. By this I mean that a half-hit tee shot could not escape the hazards, as was often possible with the rubber-cored ball. Correct driving was more appreciated in the gutty days than at the present period because of the premium placed on control. The accurate placing of the tee shot is the art of driving. Extremely long hit balls which are badly off the fairway are nothing more or less than indifferent shots. It may at once be said that the rough grass off the fairways will prove to be sufficient punishment for this mistake. This may be true, but the chief point is that the wonderful improvements in modern clubs and the more resilient ball has made recovery from the rough that much easier.

The advent of the rubber ball was instrumental in creating an entirely different method of striking the object. The solid ball required to be hit for carry, whereas it was quickly apparent that the Haskell lent itself to an enormous run. Naturally, golfers started to hit the rubber-cored ball for maximum distance. This was the start of new methods being employed in the full shots. To gain the maximum amount of run it was necessary to play for a hook. By this means, the flight of the ball was lower and the carry considerably less. The run, however, by means of the overspin that had been imparted, was twice as great and significantly longer distances were obtained. This was the beginning of the craze for length and still more length. I feel convinced, too, that it was the start of the decline in British golf.

The professionals made a determined stand against the new ball. The remaking of gutty balls was a part of the professional's business and an important source of income. Nearly all the leading players continued to use the gutty throughout the 1902 season. There were, however, one or two exceptions. Sandy Herd, the eventual winner of the 1902 Open Championship, played all four rounds with the new type of ball. Taylor, Braid and I all stuck fast to the old gutty.

Hoylake was the venue of the Open Championship in 1902. Strange as it may seem, the cause of my finishing second, one stroke behind the winner, was the Haskell ball. At the end of the first day's play, I was leading the field. I was playing as well as I could during this competition and was determined not to let a fourth Open victory slip away. However, on the second day, I was coupled with Peter McEwen, one of the few players using the rubber-cored ball. I was driving particularly well and was usually slightly ahead of my playing partner from the tee. This meant he had to play his approaches first. After seeing him pitch his ball well short of the green to allow for run, I started pitching my mashie shots short of the hole, half-expecting the gutty to run like the rubber-cored ball. I recall clearly telling myself I must not take any notice of what McEwen's ball did and that I must play my own shots up to the flag. This was easier said than done. Somehow or other I was influenced by what his ball was doing. I must have lost several shots by being short in this exasperating manner. I lost the championship by a single stroke, and I have always felt the Haskell ball unsettled me enough to cause me to lose. Nevertheless, it was not all bad that I finished as runner-up once again. My old friend Sandy Herd deserved the honour of winning the Open as much as any man who ever lived. Sandy had long been a magnificent golfer. He had, on more than one occasion, come very close to victory. There was not a stroke in the game of which he was not a master. He was a particularly fine exponent of the controlled use of pulling and slicing, and played these shots with telling effect when there was a strong wind blowing.

I had now been second in the Open Championship on the last three occasions on which it had been played. Hoylake had proved to be a severe test of golf. One of the chief reasons for this is the large number of holes on which it is possible to put the ball out of bounds. It was possibly on account of this that, although St. Andrews had at this period made a rule of stroke and distance as a penalty for out of bounds, at Hoylake the penalty was loss of distance only. It is a magnificent seaside course, but with the wind up it is as hard as any course in the world. The first hole was an exceptional two-shotter, with its out of bounds along the entire right side. I recall on one occasion in an Open Championship at Hoylake taking an eight on this hole.

In the month of January the following year, I came South and took up my duties as professional to the South Herts Golf Club at Totteridge. The Open Championship was played at Prestwick that year, 1903, and I scored my fourth victory. For reasons I will explain, my success in this championship ranks as one of the finest achievements of my life. I had for some months been far from well and, as a matter of fact, had been under the care of a doctor. I was told it would be very unwise for me to enter a big tournament.

However, I made up my mind I would play. It would not have caused me any surprise if I had been forced to retire during the competition. I was feeling weak and ill throughout the two days. I found it necessary after my morning round, both on the opening and the second day, to lay down and rest before going out in the afternoon.

My lunch consisted of a bottle of Guinness, and in the concluding round I felt so faint I thought it would be impossible for me to finish. That I was able to last until my final putt had been holed only goes to show what it is possible to accomplish under adverse circumstances. In the first round I played extremely well, and my 73 was only equalled by one other player, Sandy Herd. A 77 after lunch, with an unfortunate seven at the seventeenth, the Alps, gave me an aggregate of 150 for the thirty-six holes.

After completing my third round in 72, I was in a position to win the championship if I was able to last out the final eighteen holes. I had a lead of seven strokes over the field, and I could afford to play a safe game on this round. The real question was whether or not I could finish that last eighteen. I started out steadily and reached the turn in 37 which, under the circumstances, was better than I expected. On the homeward journey, I felt faint on several occasions. It seemed to me more than once that I would have to give up. Somehow I managed to complete the round, and when I holed out on the last green for a 78 I knew I had won the championship.

I unhesitatingly say that whatever good achievements I have accomplished, my victory in the Open Championship in 1903, under the existing circumstances, was my greatest success.

My brother Tom finished with two strong rounds of 75 and 74 to place second in the championship. I cannot repeat enough times how much I owe him and how supportive he has been to me every inch of the way. He also happens to be a very fine golfer and deserved many times over to win this championship. He is a bold player, always on the attack, and is especially deadly with his cleek.

On the day following the championship, I took part in a professional tournament promoted by the Western Gailes Club, only a few miles from Prestwick. After my trying ordeal of the previous day, which had really proved an enormous strain, it was not wise to go to Gales, but I did not wish to break my word. It had been arranged that we should play thirty-six holes under medal play conditions. My partner was James Kay of Seaton Carew, the same James Kay who had so wisely indicated at Muirfield in the 1896 Open that I should play safely on the final hole and go for a tie rather than an outright win. I was astonished at how well I played. In the morning round I scored a 68 and broke the course record, and I ended up winning the competition over Taylor and Herd with a total of 143. It did not seem possible that, feeling as I did, I could play such golf.

I returned home to Totteridge immediately after this event and had a much needed rest for a few days. I was hoping the trouble which I had experienced was now a thing of the past. Unfortunately, a relapse occurred on my home links. On the South Herts course there is a tree known as Vardon's tree which is close to the spot where I had a severe attack of haemorrhaging. After being taken home and put to bed, I was able to get up the following morning. I felt better and decided to go to the club, but on leaning forward to tie up my shoes, I had another attack of haemorrhaging. It was now clear that my health had seriously been impaired, and my doctor ordered me to a sanatorium. Thus I journeyed to Mundesley in Norfolk where I was to spend many months in an effort to recuperate.

PART II
FROM "THE COMPLETE GOLFER"

ADVICE TO BEGINNERS

I know what severe temptation there will be to all beginners to disregard the advice that I am about to offer
them; but before proceeding any further I will invite them
to take the opinion of any old golfer who, chiefly through
a careless beginning (he knows that this is the cause), has
missed his way in the golfer's life, and is still plodding
away as near the limit handicap as he was at the beginning. The beginner may perhaps be disposed to rely more
upon the statement of this man of experience and disappointment than on that of the professional, who is too
often suspected of having his own ends in view whenever
he gives advice. Let the simple question be put to him
whether, if he could be given the chance of doing it all
over again from the beginning, he would not sacrifice the
first three or six months of play to diligent study of the
principles of the game and the obtaining of some sort of
mastery over each individual shot under the careful guidance of a skilled tutor, not attempting during this time a
single complete round with all his clubs in action, and
refusing all temptations to play a single match—whether
he would not undergo this slow and perhaps somewhat
tedious period of learning if he could be almost certain of
being able at the end of it to play a really good game of
golf. I am confident that in the great majority of cases,
looking back on his misspent golfing youth, he would
answer that he would cheerfully do all this learning if he
could begin again at the beginning. Now, of course, it is
too late, for what is once learned can only with extreme
difficulty be unlearned, and it is almost impossible to reform the bad style and the bad habits which have taken
root and been cultivated in the course of many years; and
if it were possible it would be far more difficult than it
would have been to learn the game properly at the beginning.

My earnest advice to the beginner is to undergo this
slow process of tuition for nothing less than three

months, and preferably more. It is a very long time, I know, and it may seem painfully tedious work, simply knocking a ball backwards and forwards for all those months; but if he does not accept my suggestion he will have harder things to try his patience during many years afterwards, while, if he takes my advice, he may be down very near to scratch at the end of his first year, and he will be very thankful that he spent the period of probation as he did. He will be getting the finest delight out of the game that it is possible to get. It is said that the long handicap man gets as much pleasure out of the game as the short handicap man. As the former has never been a short handicap man he is evidently not qualified to judge. The scratch man, who has been through it all, would never change his scratch play for that of his old long-handicap days—at least I have never yet met the scratch man who would. No doubt the noble army of foozlers derive an immense amount of enjoyment from the practice of their game, and it is my earnest prayer that they may long continue to do so. It is one of the glorious advantages of golf that all, the skilled and the unskilled, can revel in its fascinations and mysteries; but there is no golfing delight so splendid as that which is obtained from playing well.

Now the middle-aged man may say that he is too old to go in for this sort of thing, that all he wants is a little fresh air and exercise, and as much enjoyment as he can get out of playing the game in just the same sort of way that the "other old crocks" do. He would rather play competently, of course, if it were not too late to begin; but it is too late, and there is an end of it. That is the way in which he puts it. So large a proportion of our new converts to golf belong to this middle-aged class that it is worthwhile giving a few special words of advice to them. Mr. Forty and Mr Forty-Five, you are not a day too old, and I might even make scratch men of you, if I were to take you in hand

and you did all the things I told you to do and for as long
as I told you. Given fair circumstances, there is no reason
why any man should despair of becoming either a scratch
player or one who is somewhere very near it.

So I advise every golfer to get hold of the game stroke
by stroke, and never be too ambitious at the commence-
ment. I have heard it stated on very good authority that
when Mr. Balfour first began to play he submitted himself
to very much the same process of tuition as that which I
am about to advise, and that under the guidance of Tom
Dunn he actually spent a miserable fortnight in bunkers
only, learning how to get out of them from every possible
position. The right honourable gentleman must have
saved hundreds of strokes since then as the result of that
splendid experience, trying as it must have been. He is in
these days a very good and steady player, and he might
be still better if parliamentary cares did not weigh so
heavily upon him. I may humbly suggest that the way in
which he began to play golf was characteristic of his wis-
dom.

Therefore, when the golfer has become possessed of his
first set of clubs, let him proceed to the shop of a good
professional player—presumably it will be the shop
where he bought his clubs—and let him place himself
unreservedly in the hands of this expert in the game.
Most professionals are good players and good teachers,
and the golfer cannot go far wrong in this matter if he
allows himself to be guided by his own instincts. I say that
he should place himself unreservedly in this man's hands;
but in case it should be necessary I would make one exception to this stipulation. If he thinks well of my advice
and desires to do the thing with the utmost thoroughness
from the beginning, he may request that for the first lesson or two no ball may be put upon the ground at which
to practise swings. The professional is sure to agree that
this is the best way, though he encounters so few begin-

ners who are prepared to make all the sacrifices I have
suggested, that he might have hesitated in recommending
this course of procedure himself.

A golfer's swing is often made for good or ill in the first
week of his experience. His first two days of practice may
be of the greatest importance in fashioning his style. If,
when he takes his first lesson or two and makes his first
few swings, he has a ball on the ground before him which
he is trying to hit, all his thoughts will be concentrated on
what appears to him to be the necessity of hitting it—
hitting it at any cost. No matter what he has been told
about the way to swing, he will forget it all in this moment
of anxiety, and swing anyhow. In such circumstances a
really natural and proper swing is rarely accomplished,
and, before the golfer is aware of the frightful injustice he
has done himself, his future prospects will probably have
been damaged. But if he has no ball before him he will
surely learn to swing his club in exactly the way in which
it ought to be swung. His whole mind will be concentrated upon getting every detail of the action properly
regulated and fixed according to the advice of his tutor,
and by the time he has had two lessons in this way he will
have got so thoroughly into the natural swing that, when
he comes to have a ball teed up in front of him, he will
unconsciously swing at it in the same manner as he did
when it was absent, or nearly so. The natural swing, or
some of its best features, will probably be there, although
very likely they will be considerably distorted.

At the same time the young golfer must not imagine,
because he has mastered the proper swing when there is
no ball before him, that he has overcome any considerable
portion of the difficulties of golf, for even some of the very
best players find that they can swing very much better
without a ball than with one. However, he may now taste
the sweet pleasure of driving a ball from the tee, or of
doing his best with that object in view. His initial attempts

may not be brilliant; it is more than likely that they will be sadly disappointing. He may take comfort from the fact that in ninety-nine cases out of a hundred they are so. But by and by a certain confidence will come. He will cease, under the wise advice of his tutor, to be so desperately anxious to hit the ball anyhow so long as he hits it, and then in due course the correctness of swing which he was taught in his first two days will assert itself, and the good clean-hit drives will come. There will be duffings and toppings and slicings, but one day there will be a long straight drive right away down the course, and the tyro will be told that the professional himself could not have done it better. This is one of the most pleasurable moments in life.

His system of practice thereafter should be upon the following lines. He should continue to practise diligently with his driver until he gets these good, long balls nearly every time, sternly resisting the temptation even to so much as look at any of the other nice new clubs that he has got in his bag. It may take him a week or a fortnight or a month to master the driver; but he should do it before he gives a thought to any other club. When he can use the driver with confidence, he may take out his new brassy and go through the same process with that, until he feels that on a majority of occasions, from a fairly decent lie, he could depend upon making a respectable brassy shot. He will find unsuspected difficulties in the brassy, and in doing his best to overcome them he will probably lose to some extent the facility for driving which he had acquired. Therefore, when he has become a player with his brassy, he should devote a short space of time to getting back on to his drive. It will not take him long, and then he should take out both the clubs he has been practising with and hammer away at the two of them together, until after a large amount of extra practice he finds that he is fairly reliable in driving a ball from the tee to begin with, and

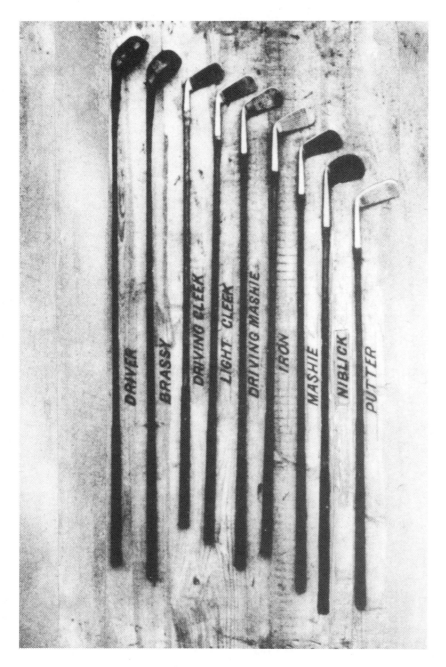

My set of clubs.

putting in a creditable second shot with his brassy from the lie upon which he found his ball.

During this second stage of learning he must deny himself the pleasure of trying his iron clubs just as rigorously as he restrained himself from the brassy when he was practising drives only; but when the driver and the brassy are doing well, he may go forward with the cleek. He will not find this learning such dull work after all. There will be something new in store for him every week, and each new club as it is taken out of the bag will afford an entirely new set of experiences. After the driver and the brassy it will be like a new game when he comes to try cleek shots, and in the same way he will persevere with the cleek until it is evident that he really knows how to use it. The driver, the brassy, and the cleek may then be practised with on the same occasion, and if he has made the best use of his time and is an apt pupil, he will find himself now and then, with these three shots taken in turn, getting beyond the green at some of the longest holes. Next it will be the turn of the iron, and so in due season he will be able to practise with the driver, the brassy, the cleek, and the iron. The mashie will follow, and then the five of them together, and at last he may have an afternoon on the green trying his skill with a putter, and listening for the first time to the music of the ball as it drops into the tin and is holed out at last.

When he has secured a fair command over all his clubs, from the driver to the niblick, the golf student may play a round of the links; but he should do so only under the watchful eye of the professional, for he will find that in thus marching on from hole to hole, and perhaps getting a little excited now and then when he plays a hole more than usually well, it is only too easy to forget all the good methods in which he has been so carefully trained and all the wise maxims he knows so well by heart that he could almost utter them in his sleep. Let him play a few rounds in this way, and in between them devote himself as assiduously as ever to practise with individual clubs, before he thinks of playing his first match. He must settle his game on a secure foundation before he measures his strength against an opponent, for unless it is thus safeguarded it is all too likely that it will crumble to ruins when the enemy is going strongly, and the novice feels, with a sense of dismay, that he is not by any means doing himself justice. Of course I am not suggesting that he should wait until he has advanced far towards perfection before he engages in his first match. When he has thoroughly grasped the principles and practice of the game, there is nothing like match play for proving his quality, but he should not be in haste thus to indulge himself. Any time from three to six months from the day when he first took a club in hand will be quite soon enough, and if he has been a careful student, and is in his first match not overcome with nerves, he should render a good account of himself and bring astonishment to the mind of his adversary when the latter is told that this is the first match of a lifetime.

During the preparatory period the golfer will be wise to limit his practices to three or four days a week. More than this will only tire him and will not be good for his game. I have only now to warn him against a constant attempt, natural but very harmful, to drive a much longer ball every time than was driven at the previous stroke. He must bring himself to understand that length comes only with experience, and that it is due to the swing becoming gradually more natural and more certain. He may see players on the links driving thirty or forty yards further than he has ever driven, and, wondering why, he is seized with a determination to hit harder, and then the old, old story of the foozled drive is told again. He forgets that these players are more experienced than he is, that their swing is more natural to them, and that they are more certain of it.

In these circumstances the extra power which they put into their stroke is natural also. To give him an exact idea of what it is that he ought to be well satisfied with, I may say that the learner who finds that he is putting just two or three yards on to his drive every second week may cease to worry about the future, for as surely as anything he will be a long driver in good time.

THE DRIVE
AND THE GRIP

It has been said that the amateur golfers of Great Britain are in these days suffering from a "debauchery of long driving." The general sense of Mr. Travis's remark is excellent, meaning that there is a tendency to regard a very long drive as almost everything in the playing of a hole, and to be utterly careless of straightness and the short game so long as the ball has been hit from the tee to the full extent of the golfer's power. A long drive is not by any means everything, and the young golfer should resist any inclination to strive for the 250-yard ball to the detriment or even the total neglect of other equally important, though perhaps less showy, considerations in the playing of a hole. But having said so much, and conveyed the solemn warning that is necessary, I am obliged to admit that the long driver has very full justification for himself, and that the wisely regulated ambition of the young player to be one is both natural and laudable. The long drive, as I say, is not everything; but to play well it is as necessary to make a good drive as to hole a short putt, or nearly so, and from the golfer who does not drive well a most marvellous excellence is required in the short game if he is to hold his own in good company, or ever be anything more than a long-handicap man. The good drive is the foundation of a good game, and just as one and one make two, so it follows that the man who drives the longer ball has the rest of the game made easier and more certain for him. There is no stroke in golf that gives the same amount of pleasure as does the perfect driving of the ball from the tee, none that makes the heart feel lighter, and none that seems to bring the glow of delight into the watching eye as this one does.

Let us get on to our drive.

In the first place, the driver must be selected, and the hints I have already given upon the choice of clubs will serve tolerably well in this respect. Let it only be said again that the golfer should do his utmost to avoid extremes in length or shortness. One hears of the virtues of fishing-rod drivers, and the next day that certain great players display a tendency to shorten their clubs. There is nothing like the happy medium, which has proved its capability of getting the longest balls. The length of the club must, of course, vary according to the height of the player, for what would be a short driver for a six-foot man would almost be a fishing-rod to the diminutive person who stands but five feet high. Let the weight be medium also; but for reasons already stated do not let it err on the side of lightness. The shaft of the club should be of moderate suppleness. As I have said, if it is too whippy it may be hard to control, but if it is too stiff it leaves too much hard work to be done by the muscles of the golfer. Practising what I preach, my own drivers are carefully selected for this delicate medium of suppleness of shaft, and when a stick is found that is exactly perfect it is well worth great care forever. Also I reiterate that the head of the club should not be too large; driving is not thereby made any easier, and carelessness is encouraged. The face should not be quite vertical: if it were, only the top edge and not the full face would be seen when the stance had been taken and the club head was resting upon the tee in its proper place. There must be just so much loft that the face can be seen when the golfer is ready and in position for the swing. But avoid having too much loft filed on the club as a fancied remedy for driving too low and getting into all the bunkers. You do not fail to get the ball up because there is not sufficient loft on the club, but because you are doing something wrong which can easily be remedied; while, on the other hand, be very careful of the fact that, as you add loft to the face of the driver, so at the same time you are cutting off distance and losing both power and the delightful sense of it.

Tee the ball low, rejecting the very prevalent but erroneous idea that you are more certain of getting it away cleanly and well when it is poised high off the ground. The stroke that sweeps the ball well away from the low tee is the most natural and perfect, and it follows that the ball, properly driven from this low tee, is the best of all. Moreover, one is not so liable to get too much underneath the ball and make a feeble shot into the sky, which is one of the most exasperating forms of ineffectual effort in the whole range of golf. Another convincing argument in favour of the low tee is that it preserves a greater measure of similarity between the first shot and the second, helping to make the latter, with the brassy, almost a repetition of the first, and therefore simple and comparatively easy. If you make a high tee, when you come to play your second stroke with your brassy, you will be inclined to find fault with even the most perfect brassy lies. As I have already suggested, one of the principles of my long game is to make the play with the brassy as nearly similar to that with the driver as possible, and a low tee is the first step in that direction.

Then, as to distance from the ball. The player should stand so far away from it that when he is in position and the club face is resting against the teed ball, just as when ready to strike it, the end of the shaft shall reach exactly up to his left knee when the latter is ever so slightly bent. In this position he should be able, when he has properly gripped the club, to reach the ball comfortably and without any stretching, the arms indeed being not quite straight out but having a slight bend at the elbows, so that when the club is waggled in the preliminary address to the ball, plenty of play can be felt in them.

It will be noticed, in the first place, that I have my toes turned well outwards. The pivoting which is necessary, and which will be described in due course, is done naturally and without any effort when the toes are pointed in this manner. While it is a mistake to place the feet too near each other, there is a common tendency to place them too

The stance for the driver and the brassy.

far apart. When this is done, ease and perfection of the swing are destroyed and power is wasted, whilst the whole movement is devoid of grace. It will be seen that my left foot is a little, but not much, in advance of the ball. My left heel, indeed, is almost level with it. The right foot is in advance of the left, so that at the most critical period of the stroke there shall be nothing to impede the follow-through but everything to encourage it, and so that at the finish the body itself can be thrown forward in the last effort to continue the application of power. It would not be in a position to do so if the left foot were in front to bar the way. The position of the ball as between the right foot and the left is such that the club will strike it just at the time when it is capable of doing so to the utmost advantage, being then, and for the split second during which ball and club remain in contact, moving in a straight line and at maximum speed.

Now comes the all-important consideration of the grip. This is another matter in which the practice of golfers differs greatly, and upon which there has been much controversy. My grip is one of my own invention. It differs materially from most others, and if I am asked to offer any excuse for it, I shall say that I adopted it only after a careful trial of all the other grips of which I had ever heard, that in theory and practice I find it admirable—more so than any other—and that in my opinion it has contributed materially to the attainment of such skill as I possess. The favour which I accord to my method might be viewed with suspicion if it had been my natural or original grip, which came naturally or accidentally to me when I first began to play as a boy, so many habits that are bad being contracted at this stage and clinging to the player for the rest of his life. But this was not the case, for when I first began to play golf I grasped my club in what is generally regarded as the orthodox manner, that is to

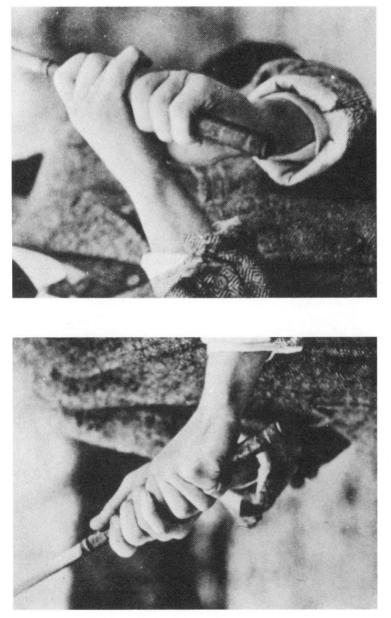

The overlapping grip.

say, across the palms of both hands separately, with both thumbs right round the shaft and with the joins between the thumbs and first fingers showing like two V's over the top of the shaft. This is usually described as the two-V or palm grip, and it is the one which is taught by the majority of professionals. Of course it is beyond question that some players achieve very fine results with this grip, but I abandoned it many years ago in favour of one that I consider to be better. My contention is that this grip of mine is sounder in theory and easier in practice, tends to make a better stroke and to secure a straighter ball, and that players who adopt it from the beginning will stand a much better chance of driving well at an early stage than if they went in for the old-fashioned two-V. My grip is an overlapping, but not an interlocking one. I use it for all my strokes, and it is only when putting that I vary it in the least, and then the change is so slight as to be scarcely noticeable.

It will be seen at once that I do not grasp the club across the palm of either hand. The club being taken in the left hand first, the shaft passes from the knuckle joint of the first finger across the ball of the second. The left thumb lies straight down the shaft—that is to say, it is just to the right of the centre of the shaft. But the following are the significant features of the grip. The right hand is brought up so high that the palm of it covers the left thumb, leaving very little of the latter to be seen. The first and second fingers of the right hand just reach round to the thumb of the left, and the third finger completes the overlapping process, so that the club is held in the grip as if it were in a vice. The little finger of the right hand rides on the first finger of the left. The great advantage of this grip is that both hands feel and act like one, and if, even while sitting in his chair, a player who has never tried it before will take a stick in his hands in the manner I have described, he must at once be convinced that there is a great deal in

what I say for it, although, of course, if he has been accustomed to the two V's, the success of my grip cannot be
guaranteed at the first trial. It needs some time to become
thoroughly happy with it.

We must now consider the degree of tightness of the
grip by either hand, for this is an important matter. Some
teachers of golf and various books of instruction inform us
that we should grasp the club firmly with the left hand
and only lightly with the right, leaving the former to do
the bulk of the work and the other merely to guide the
operations. It is astonishing with what persistency this
error has been repeated, for error I truly believe it is. Ask
any really first-class player with what comparative tightness he holds the club in his right and left hands, and I am
confident that in nearly every case he will declare that he
holds it nearly if not quite as tightly with the right hand as
with the left. Personally I grip quite as firmly with the
right hand as with the left. When the other way is
adopted, the left hand being tight and the right hand
simply watching it, as it were, there is an irresistible tendency for the latter to tighten up suddenly at some part of
the upward or downward swing, and when it does, so
there will be mischief. Depend upon it, the instinct of
activity will prevent the right hand from going through
with the swing in that indefinite state of looseness. Perhaps a yard from the ball in the upward swing, or a yard
from it when coming down, there will be a convulsive
grip of the right hand which, with an immediate acknowl-
edgment of guilt, will relax again. Such a happening is
usually fatal; it certainly deserves to be. Slicing, pulling,
sclaffing—all these tragedies may at times be traced to this
determination of the right hand not to be ignored but to
have its part in the hitting of the drive. Therefore in all
respects my right hand is a joint partner with the left.

The grip with the first finger and thumb of my right
hand is exceedingly firm, and the pressure of the little

finger on the knuckle of the left hand is very decided. In
the same way, it is the thumb and first finger of the left
hand that have most of the gripping work to do. Again,
the palm of the right hand presses hard against the thumb
of the left. In the upward swing this pressure is gradually
decreased, until when the club reaches the turning-point
there is no longer any such pressure; indeed, at this point
the palm and the thumb are barely in contact. This release
is a natural one, and will or should come naturally to the
player for the purpose of allowing the head of the club to
swing well and freely back. But the grip of the thumb and
first finger of the right hand, as well as that of the little
finger upon the knuckle of the first finger of the left hand,
is still as firm as at the beginning. As the club head is
swung back again towards the ball, the palm of the right
hand and the thumb of the left gradually come together
again. Both the relaxing and the re-tightening are done
with the most perfect graduation, so that there shall be no
jerk to take the club off the straight line. The easing begins
when the hands are about shoulder high and the club
shaft is perpendicular, because it is at this time that the
club begins to pull, and if it were not let out in the manner
explained, the result would certainly be a half shot or very
little more than that, for a full and perfect swing would be
an impossibility. This relaxation of the palm also serves to
give more freedom to the wrist at the top of the swing just
when that freedom is desirable.

I have the strongest belief in the soundness of the grip
that I have thus explained, for when it is employed both
hands are acting in unison and to the utmost advantage,
whereas it often happens in the two-V grip, even when
practised by the most skilfull players, that in the downward swing there is a sense of the left hand doing its
utmost to get through and of the right hand holding it
back.

There is only one other small matter to mention in connection with the question of grip. Some golfers imagine that if they rest the left thumb down the shaft and let the right hand press upon it there will be a considerable danger of breaking the thumb, so severe is the pressure when the stroke is being made. As a matter of fact, I have quite satisfied myself that if the thumb is kept in the same place there is not the slightest risk of anything of the kind. Also if the thumb remains immovable, as it should, there is no possibility of the club turning in the hands as so often happens in the case of the two-V grip when the ground is hit rather hard, a pull or a slice being the usual consequence. I must be excused for treating upon these matters at such length. They are often neglected, but they are of extreme importance in laying the foundations of a good golf game.

A waggle of the head of the club as a preliminary before commencing the swing is sometimes necessary after the stance and grip have taken, but every young golfer should be warned against excess in this habit. With the stance and grip arranged, the line of the shot in view, and a full knowledge of what is required from the stroke, there is really very little more that needs thinking about before the swing is taken. One short preliminary waggle will tend to make the player feel comfortable and confident, but some golfers may be observed trying the patience of all about them by an interminable process of waggling, the most likely result of which is a duffed shot, since, when at last the stroke is made, the player is in a state of semi-catalepsy, and has no clear idea of what he is going to do or how he is going to do it.

THE SWING

Now let us consider the upward and downward swings of the club, and the movements of the arms, legs, feet, and body in relation to them. As a first injunction, it may be stated that the club should be drawn back rather more slowly than you intend to bring it down again. "Slow back" is a golfing maxim that is both old and wise. The club should begin to gain speed when the upward swing is about half made, and the increase should be gradual until the top is reached, but it should never be so fast that control of the club is to any extent lost at the turning-point. The head of the club should be taken back fairly straight from the ball for the first six inches, and after that any tendency to sweep it round sharply to the back should be avoided. Keep it very close to the straight line until it is half-way up. The old St. Andrews style of driving largely consisted in this sudden sweep round, but the modern method appears to be easier and productive of better results. So this carrying of the head of the club upwards and backwards seems to be a very simple matter, capable of explanation in a very few words; but, as every golfer of a month's experience knows, there is a long list of details to be attended to, which I have not yet named, each of which seems to vie with the others in its attempt to destroy the effectiveness of the drive.

The head should be kept perfectly motionless from the time of the address until the ball has been sent away and is well on its flight. The least deviation from this rule means a proportionate danger of disaster. When a drive has been badly foozled, the readiest and most usual explanation is that the eye has been taken off the ball, and the wise old men who have been watching shake their heads solemnly and utter that parrot-cry of the links, "Keep your eye on the ball." Certainly this is a good and necessary rule so far as it goes; but I do not believe that one drive in a hundred is missed because the eye has not been kept on the ball. On the other hand, I believe that one of the basic causes of

failure with the tee shot is the moving of the head. Until
the ball has gone, it should, as I say, be as nearly perfectly
still as possible, and I would have written that it should not
be moved to the extent of a sixteenth of an inch, but for the
fact that it is not human to be so still. When the head has
been kept quite still and the club has reached the top of the
upward swing, the eyes should be looking over the middle
of the left shoulder, the left eye being dead over the centre
of that shoulder.

In the upward swing the right shoulder should be
raised gradually. It is unnecessary for me to submit any
instruction on this point, since the movement is natural
and inevitable, and there is no tendency towards excess;
but the arms and wrists need attention. From the moment
when the club is first taken back, the left wrist should
begin to turn inwards, and so turn away the face of the
club from the ball. When this is properly done, the toe of
the club will point to the sky when it is level with the
shoulder and will be dead over the middle of the shaft.
This turning or twisting process continues all the way
until at the top of the swing the toe of the club is pointing
straight downwards to the ground.

During the upward swing the arms should be gradually
let out in the enjoyment of perfect ease and freedom until
at the top of the swing the left arm, from the shoulder to
the elbow, is gently touching the body, while the right
arm is up above it and almost level with the club.

In the upward movement of the club the body must
pivot from the waist alone, and there must be no swaying
not even to the extent of an inch. When the player sways
in his drive, the stroke he makes is a body stroke pure and
simple. The body is trying to do the work the arms should
do.

The movements of the feet and legs are important. In
addressing the ball you stand with both feet flat and se-
curely placed on the ground, the weight equally divided

between them, and the legs so slightly bent at the knee joints as to make the bending scarcely noticeable. This position is maintained during the upward movement of the club until the arms begin to pull at the body. The easiest and most natural thing to do then, and the one which suggests itself, is to raise the heel of the left foot and begin to pivot on the left toe, which allows the arms to proceed with their uplifting process without let or hindrance. Do not begin to pivot on the left toe ostentatiously, or because you feel you ought to do so, but only when you know the time has come and you want to, and do it only to such an extent that the club can reach the full extent of the swing without any difficulty.

Be careful not to dwell at the turn of the swing. The club has been gaining in speed right up to this point, and though I suppose that, theoretically, there is a pause at the turning-point, lasting for an infinitesimal portion of a second, the golfer should scarcely be conscious of it. He must be careful to avoid a sudden jerk, but if he dwells at the top of the stroke for only a second, or half that short period of time, his upward swing in all its perfection will have been completely wasted, and his stroke will be made under precisely the same circumstances and with exactly the same disadvantages as if the club had been poised in this position at the start and there had been no attempt at swinging of any description. In such circumstances a long ball is an impossibility, and a straight one a matter of exceeding doubt. The odds are not very greatly in favour of the ball being rolled off the teeing ground. So don't dwell at the turn; come back again with the club.

The club should gradually gain in speed from the moment of the turn until it is in contact with the ball, so that at the moment of impact its head is travelling at its fastest pace. After the impact, the club head should be allowed to follow the ball straight in the line of the flag as far as the arms will let it go, and then, having done everything that

The top of the swing.

is possible, it swings itself out at the other side of the shoulders. The entire movement must be perfectly smooth and rhythmical; in the downward swing, while the club is gaining speed, there must not be the semblance of a jerk anywhere such as would cause a jump, or a double swing, or what might be called a cricket stroke. That, in a few lines, is the whole story of the downward swing, but it needs some elaboration. In the first place, avoid the tendency—which is to some extent natural—to let the arms go out or away from the body as soon as the downward movement begins. When they are permitted to do so, the club head escapes from its proper line, and a fault is committed which cannot be remedied before the ball is struck. Knowing by instinct that you are outside the proper course, you make a great effort at correction, the face of the club is drawn across the ball, and there is one more slice. The arms should be kept fairly well in during the latter half of the downward swing, both elbows almost grazing the body. If they are properly attended to when the club is going up, there is much more likelihood of their coming down all right.

The head is still kept motionless and the body pivots easily at the waist; but when the club is half-way down, the left hip is allowed to go forward a little—a preliminary to and preparation for the forward movement of the body which is soon to begin. The weight is being gradually moved back again from the right leg to the left. At the moment of impact both feet are equally weighted and are flat on the ground, just as they were when the ball was being addressed; indeed, the position of the body, legs, arms, head, and every other detail is, or ought to be, exactly the same when the ball is being struck as when it was addressed, and for that reason I refer my readers again to the photograph of the address as the most correct position of everything at the moment of striking. After the impact the weight is thrown on to the left leg, which

The finish.

stiffens, while the right toe pivots and the knee bends just as its partner did in the earlier stage of the stroke, but perhaps to a greater extent, since there is no longer any need for restraint.

Now pay attention to the wrists. They should be held fairly tightly. If the club is held tightly, the wrists will be tight, and *vice versa*. When the wrists are tight there is little play in them, and more is demanded of the arms. I don't believe in the long ball coming from the wrists. In defiance of principles which are accepted in many quarters, I will go so far as to say that, except in putting, there is no pure wrist shot in golf.

When the ball has been struck, and the follow-through is being accomplished, there are two rules, hitherto held sacred, which may at last be broken. With the direction and force of the swing, your chest is naturally turned round until it is facing the flag, and your body now abandons all restraint, and to a certain extent throws itself, as it were, after the ball. There is a great art in timing this body movement exactly. If it takes place the fiftieth part of a second too soon, the stroke will be entirely ruined; if it comes too late, it will be quite ineffectual and will only result in making the golfer feel uneasy and as if something had gone wrong. When made at the proper instant it adds a good piece of distance to the drive, and that instant, as explained, is just when the club is following through. When the ball has gone, and the arms, following it, begin to pull, the head, which has so far been held perfectly still, is lifted up so as to give freedom to the swing, and incidentally it allows the eyes to follow the flight of the ball.

I like to see the arms finish well up, with the hands level with the head. This generally means a properly hit ball and a good follow-through. At the finish of the stroke the arms should be as nearly as possible level with each other.

THE BRASSY
AND THE SPOON

When to your caddie you say, "Give me my brassy," it is a sign that there is serious work to be done—as serious and anxious as any that has to be accomplished during the six or seven minutes' journey from the tee to the hole. Many golfers have a fondness for the brassy greater even than for the driver, and the brassy shot when well played certainly affords a greater sense of satisfaction than the drive—great as is the joy of a good drive—because one is conscious of having triumphed over difficulties. When the ball is lying well and it has to be played to the green, the driver is naturally taken, but when the lie is low, the brassy is called for, so that an effort may be made to pick the ball up cleanly. The stroke with the brassy must always be first-class. One that is a little inferior to the best may place the player in serious difficulties. On the other hand, the brassy seldom flatters its user, though in the hands of a master player it is perhaps the club that will gain a stroke for him more often than any other, the last bunker being surmounted and the green reached without any need for a short approach with an iron club. Therefore, the golfer must make up his mind to attain excellence with the brassy, for mediocrity with it will always handicap him severely.

I have already insisted that the method of play, the stance, the swing, and all the rest of it should be the same with the brassy as with the driver. I do not believe in allowing the slightest difference, the only result of which can be to increase the difficulty of the brassy shot. Given a ball through the green lying fairly well, a level piece of earth to stand upon, and a practically unlimited distance to be played, then the brassy stroke is absolutely identical with the drive, and if the ball is sufficiently well teed, or its lie is clean enough, there is no reason whatever why the driver should not be taken for the stroke. Obviously, however, as the lie which you get for your second shot depends on chance, and must be taken as it is found,

there are times when a variation from the standard
method of driving will be necessary, and it is to the process of play on these occasions that I shall chiefly direct
my remarks in this chapter.

First, however, as to the brassy itself. Its shaft should be
slightly stiffer than that of the driver, for it has much
harder and rougher work to accomplish, for which the
whippy stick of a slender driver would be too frail. In a
desperate case, when the ball is lying in an apparently
impossible place, the brassy is sometimes taken, in the
hope that the best may happen and the situation be
saved. That is why the brassy has a sole of brass which
will cut away obstructions behind the ball as the head of
the club is swept on to it. It often happens that you must
hit, as it were, an inch or two behind the ball in order to
get it up. Therefore let the shaft be strong. It should be
exactly the same length as that of the driver, and not a half
inch or an inch shorter, as is often recommended. I do not
accept any argument in favour of the shorter shaft. The
golfer having driven from the tee needs to be persuaded
that he has again what is practically a driving shot to make
for his second, and thus to be imbued with that feeling of
experience and confidence which makes for success.
When the clubs are of the same length there is equal fa-
miliarity in using them; but if he is given a shorter club to
play his brassy shot with, he feels that there is something
of a novel nature to be done. The face of the brassy should
be a little shorter than that of the driver, to permit of its
being worked into little depressions in which the ball may
be lying; but this variation of the construction of the head
should not be carried to excess. Obviously there needs to
be more loft on the face of the club than on that of the
driver.

The stance for the brassy stroke is generally the same as
for the drive. If the player feels it to be desirable, he may
stand an inch or two nearer to the ball, and perhaps as

much behind the ball when he wishes to get well underneath so as to lift it up. The swing should be the same,
save that more care should be taken to ensure the grip
with the hands being quite tight, for as the club head
comes into contact with the turf before taking the ball, the
club may turn in the hands and cause a slice or pull unless
perfect control be kept over it.

A more important question is where and how to hit the
ball. If it is lying fairly well, it is only necessary to skim the
top of the turf and take it cleanly. There is no necessity in
such a case, as is too often imagined by inexperienced
players, to delve down into the turf so that the ball may be
lifted up. If the stroke is played naturally, in the way I
have indicated, the loft on the face of the brassy is quite
sufficient to give the necessary amount of rise to the ball
as it leaves the club. But if, as so often happens, the ball
is just a trifle cupped, a different attitude must be adopted
towards it. It is now desired that the club should come
down to the turf about an inch behind the ball, and with
this object in view the eyes should be directed to that
point. When the club is swung down on to that spot, its
head will plough through the turf and be well under the
ball by the time it reaches it, and the desired rise will
follow. Swing in the same manner as for the drive. The
commonest fault in the playing of this stroke comes from
the instinct of the player to try to scoop out the ball from
its resting-place, and in obedience to this instinct down
goes the right shoulder when the club is coming on to the
ball. In the theory of the beginner this course of procedure
may seem wise and proper, but he will inevitably be disappointed with the result, and in time he will come to
realise that all attempts to scoop must fail. What the club
cannot do in the ordinary way when pushed through the
turf, as I have indicated, cannot be done at all, and it is
dangerous to the stroke and dangerous to one's game to
trifle with the grand principles.

The man with the spoon is coming back again to the links, and this seems to be the most convenient opportunity for a few remarks on play with this club—the baffy, as it is frequently called. One rarely mentions the spoon without being reminded of the difficulty as to the nomenclature of golf which beset a certain Frenchman on his first introduction to the game. "They zay to me," he complained, "'Will you take ze tee?' and I answer, 'Ah, oui,' but they give me no tea, but make a leetle hill with the sand. Then they zay, 'Will you take the spoon?' They have give me no tea, but no matter. I answer again, 'Ah, oui, monsieur,' but they give no spoon either. So I give up the thought of the tea, and play with the new club that they do give to me."

The method of play with the spoon is very much the same as with the brassy, with only such modifications as are apparently necessary. For example, the club being shorter, the feet will be placed slightly nearer to the ball; and although the baffy calls for a fairly long swing, the player will find that he is naturally indisposed to take the club head so far around his back as he was with the longer wooden clubs. In other respects, the upward and downward swing, the grip, the follow-through, and everything else are the same.

THE CLEEK AND
THE PUSH SHOT

It is high time we came to consider the iron clubs that
are in our bag. His play with the irons is a fine test of the
golfer. It calls for extreme skill and delicacy, and the man
who is surest with these implements is generally surest of
his match. The fathers of golf had no clubs with metal
heads, and for a long time after they came into use there
was a lingering prejudice against them; but in these days
there is no man so bold as to say that any long hole can
always be played so well with wood all through as with a
mixture of wood and iron in the proper proportions. It
may be, as we are often told, that the last improvement in
iron clubs has not yet been made; but I must confess that
the tools now at the disposal of the golfer come as near to
my ideal of the best for their purpose as I can imagine any
tools to do, and no golfer is at liberty to blame the club-
maker for his own incapacity on the links, though it may
frequently happen that his choice and taste in the matter
of his golfing goods are at fault. There are many varieties
of every class of iron clubs, and their gradations of
weight, of shape, of loft, and of all their other features are
delicate almost to the point of invisibility; but the old
golfer who has an affection for a favourite club knows
when another which he handles differs from it to the extent of a single point in these gradations.

My favourite iron club is the cleek, the most powerful
and generally useful of them all, though one which is
much abused and often called hard names. If you wish,
you may drive a very long ball with a cleek, and if the
spirit moves you so to do you may wind up the play at the
hole by putting with it too. But these after all are what I
may call its unofficial uses, for the club has its own particular duties, and for the performance of them there is no
adequate substitute. Therefore, when a golfer says, as
misguided golfers sometimes do, that he cannot play with
the cleek, that he gets equal or superior results with other
clubs, and that therefore he has abandoned it to perma-

nent seclusion in the locker, you may shake your head at him, for he is only deceiving himself. Like the wares of boastful advertisers, there is no other which is "just as good," and if a golfer finds that he can do no business with his cleek, the sooner he learns to do it, the better will it be for his game.

Now we may examine the peculiarities of play with the cleek. It will be found that the shaft of the cleek is usually some two to four inches shorter than the driver, and this circumstance in itself is sufficient to demand a considerable modification in the stance and method of use. The left foot should be brought more forward into line with the right, but it is still behind it, and it is essential that it should be so, in order that the arms may be allowed a free passage through after the stroke. The feet remain about the same distance apart, but it should be noticed that the whole body has been moved forward some four inches in relation to the ball. The stance in the case of all iron clubs should be studied with great care, for a half inch the wrong way seems to have a much greater power for evil than it does in the case of wooden clubs.

I do not favour a really full shot either with the cleek or any other iron club. When the limit of capability is demanded with this or most other iron clubs in the bag, it is time to consider whether a wooden instrument should not be employed. Therefore I very seldom play the full cleek shot, but limit myself to one which may be said to be slightly above the three-quarters. This is usually quite sufficient for all purposes of length, and it is easier with this limit of swing to keep the wrists and the club generally more under control.

There is a shot with the cleek which will take many weeks of arduous practice to master. In my opinion, it is one of the most valuable and telling shots in golf, and it is called the push shot. Of all the strokes that I like to play, this is my favourite. It is a half shot, but as a matter of fact almost as much length can be obtained with it as in any other way. It is a somewhat peculiar shot, and must be played very exactly. In the first place, either a shorter cleek (about two inches shorter, and preferably with a little more loft than the driving cleek possesses) should be used, or the other one must be gripped lower down the handle. The stance is taken much nearer to the ball than when an ordinary cleek shot is played. The right foot is nearer to the ball, and the body and feet have again been moved a trifle to the left. Moreover, it is recommended that in the address the hands should be held a little more forward than usual. In this half shot the club is not swung so far back, nor is the follow-through continued so far at the finish. To make a complete success of this stroke, the ball must be hit in much the same manner as when a low ball is wanted in driving against the wind. In playing an ordinary cleek shot, the turf is grazed before the ball in the usual manner, but to execute the push shot perfectly, the sight should be directed to

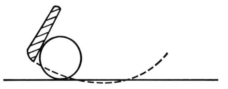

The push shot with the cleek.

the centre of the ball, and the club should be brought directly on to it. In this way the turf should be grazed an inch or two on the far side of the ball. The diagram on this page shows the passage of the club through the ball. Then not only is the ball kept low, but certain peculiarities are imparted to its flight, which are of the utmost value. Not only may the ball be depended upon never to rise above a certain height, but, having reached its highest point, it seems to come down very quickly, travelling but a few yards more and having very little run on it. When this shot is mastered, a long approach shot can be gauged with splendid accuracy. The ball is sent forwards and upwards until it is almost overhanging the green, and then down it comes close to the pin. I admit that when the ball is hit in this way the shot is made rather difficult—though not so difficult as it looks—and, of course, it is not absolutely imperative that this method should be followed.

Some good players make the stroke in the same way as the full shot, so far as hitting the ball is concerned, but in doing so they certainly lose the advantages I have pointed out and stand less chance of scoring through a finely placed ball. I may remark that personally I play not only my half cleek stroke but all my cleek strokes in this way, so much am I devoted to the qualities of flight which are thereby imparted to the ball, and though I do not insist that others should do likewise in all cases, I am certainly of opinion that they are missing something when they do not learn to play the half shot in this manner. The greatest danger they have to fear is that in their too conscious efforts to keep the club clear of the ground until after the impact, they will overdo it and simply top the ball. I suggest that when this stroke is being practised a close watch should be kept over the forearms and wrists, which do most of the work. The arms should be kept well in, and the wrists should be very tight and firm. The shot is played to greatest advantage on a hard and fairly dry course.

Many people are inclined to ask why, instead of playing a half shot with the cleek, another iron is not taken and a full stroke made with it. For some reason which I cannot explain, there seems to be an enormous number of players who prefer a full shot with any club to a half shot with another. Why is it that they like to swing so much and waste so much power, unmindful of the fact that the

The finish of a push shot.

shorter the swing the greater the accuracy? The principle of my own game, which I always impress upon others when I have an opportunity, is, "Reach the hole in the easiest way you can." The easier way is generally the surer way. When, therefore, there is a choice between a full shot with one club or a half shot with another, I invariably prefer the half shot. I should always play the half cleek shot in preference to the full iron, because, to my mind, it is easier and safer, and because there is less danger of the ball skidding off the club.

PART III
FROM "HOW TO PLAY GOLF"

CHAPTER VIII
ON THE GREEN

ON THE GREEN

Putting is a delicate matter, and I, of all people, ought to write about it in a delicate way. The reader of this book who has honoured me by noticing my doings on the links during recent years, and has observed my infinite capacity for missing little putts, may arrive at the conclusion that I lack nothing in presumptuousness when I offer instruction as to the best way of getting the ball into the hole from a short distance. Except, however, for emphasizing a few fundamental truths which are immutably correct, I do not intend to tell anybody how to putt. There are many ways of performing the operation successfully. I can claim, however, to be in a position to explain how not to putt. I think I know as well as anybody how not to do it.

Putting is, in a sense, a pastime distinct from golf. Half the secret of accomplishing it triumphantly lies, I suppose, in realizing that it is not very difficult. When driving or approaching, it is necessary for the player to remember certain established principles, and follow them to the letter if he would produce the desired result. There is one valuable precept which applies to putting as strongly as to any other shot in the game. That maxim is: "Keep the head still." As regards stance and manner of hitting the ball, it is for the individual to discover on the green the means that suit him best with the club that gives him most confidence. The finest way to putt is the way that gets the ball into the hole. And confidence is half the battle. Without it, putting is not merely difficult; it is impossible.

The reader may not need to be reminded that, of late years, I have often been lacking in confidence on the greens. Especially has this been the case in connexion with downright easy putts—those varying in length from six inches to four or five feet. Let me unburden my soul; let me relate just what I have done wrongly on hundreds of occasions, just why I have done it, and just how I have sought to cure myself—sought with some success, if I may judge by my putting during the period in which this book was written.

Perhaps it will be best if I reverse the order of the ordeal, and start with the cure. On occasions I have gone on to the course in the rapidly gathering gloom, when, in playing even a short putt, the character of the ground between the ball and the hole has been hard to distinguish. I have seen the ball and the hole; and found that I could nearly always put the former into the latter—simply because, it seemed to me, I had not worried to search for intervening difficulties. If the golfer will adjourn to a green to practise putting in the dusk of an evening, I feel sure that he will find the whole business much easier than it seems in the daytime. With light just sufficient to enable him to detect the dim outlines of the slopes, but not enough to give him the opportunity of exaggerating their horrors, he will discover himself putting with self-reliance and success. Care is essential; but I firmly believe that, if you feel anxious and are determined to look diligently for complications along the line, you will find them even though they have no existence outside your own mind.

That remark, however, merely serves to accentuate the inner peculiarity of putting, and its difference from any other department of the game. In drives and iron shots, there are degrees of prosperity. You may not hit your drive quite properly, but you may still be on the course without serious loss of distance. The fate of a short putt is an extreme; it is either perfect or ghastly. There is no mediocrity, no chance of recovery. That is why, I presume, the stroke is so trying; it is so fateful. To be able to appreciate its intricacies at precisely their correct value, and treat them accordingly, is one of the secrets of successful putting. They must not be underrated, because sometimes they really are serious; but when they insist upon presenting themselves in a portentous way, the poor victim is a person to be pitied. They get on his nerves to such an extent that he simply cannot keep his head still during the stroke. And so he fails. In the dusk, when the survey of the line in minute detail is impossible, putting really is easy. At least, so I have found it. It is a strange remedy to get out in the gloom in order to obtain confidence, but it is no stranger than the disease.

I suppose that, at some time or other, nearly everybody has suffered from incapacity within four feet of the hole. In my own case, the attack was painfully protracted; I can only hope that I am justified in speaking of it now in the past tense. I have never felt nervous when taking part in a golf tournament; this lack of confidence which overtook me when I played a short putt was something altogether worse than nervousness. As I stood addressing the ball, I would watch for my right hand to jump. At the end of about two seconds, I would not be looking at the ball at all. My gaze would have become riveted on my right hand. I simply could not resist the desire to discover what it was going to do. Directly I felt that it was about to jump, I would snatch at the ball in a desperate effort to play the shot before the involuntary movement could take effect. Up would go my head and body with a start, and off would go the ball—anywhere but on the proper line. Such was the outcome of a loss of confidence. I felt completely comfortable with putts of three yards or more, and could play them satisfactorily; it was when I got to within four feet of the hole that I became conscious of the difficulties, studied the line with infinite particularity so as to leave nothing to chance, and then watched my hand to see what it was going to do. I could always tell when I was about to have relief. If no jump visited me on the first green, I knew that I was safe for the round. As a generator of confidence, I would recommend a course of putting in the dusk. There is a lot of imagination in seeing a line all the way from the ball to the hole.

Unquestionably the most important principle in putting

is to keep the head and body absolutely still during the stroke. I know this from bitter experience. Whenever I have been putting badly, I have been moving my head (and therefore my body), and I am sure that the great majority of failures on the green are traceable to the same fault. The arms and wrists should make the club act as a pendulum. The implement should swing easily without causing the body to move to the extent of even an eighth of an inch. If the clock swayed to and fro with the pendulum, it would not, I imagine, keep very good time. When you are putting, your head should be as still as the dial of the clock; your body should be as stable as the case. Your arms, wrists, and club should constitute the pendulum. Then you will keep good time. The methods of all good putters demonstrate the truth of this assertion—all, at least, save one. The inevitable exception to the rule is Tom Ball, who certainly does sway to some extent during the stroke. As he brings the club forward, his head and body move in the same direction, with the result that his left hip, which starts behind the ball, is in front of the object by the time that he plays the shot. Tom Ball is a very fine putter, and any golfer who possesses a characteristic on the green such as that described, and who thrives on it, is justified in his unorthodoxy. There is no truer saying than that putting is an inspiration, and it is certain that we do not all adopt the same pose in moments of inspiration. Consequently let the player putt in the way that suits him; the point that I am trying to emphasize is that it is not much use for the average golfer to try this body movement. In ninety-nine persons out of a hundred, it would be fatal.

Accurate judgment of strength comes with practice; the chief difficulty is to make the ball travel in the proper direction. In nearly all cases, the missing of short putts is caused by the moving of the head. If you can summon the determination to continue looking at the spot where the

ball has been for a second or two after you have struck it,
you will not often miss a short putt. But the accomplishment of that feat of restraint simply means that you are
possessed of confidence; it means that you know that the
ball has gone into the hole, so that you are not in a hurry
to gaze at the result. The best way to encourage this com-
forting faith is to keep the head down till the finish of the
follow-through.

Twelve or fifteen years ago, when putting never gave
me the slightest trouble, I always played on the green a
stroke which was simply a condensed form of the push-
shot. I addressed the ball with the hands very slightly in
front of it, imparted back-spin to it by the use of the
wrists, and grazed the grass several inches in front of the
spot from which the ball had been struck. That was when
I employed a putting-cleek for the business. With the skit-
tish rubber-cored ball, I do not fancy the push-shot on the
green. I endeavour to play a pendulum stroke, which in-
duces a steady follow-through with the arms—not the
body.

The choice of grip, like that of club, must be a matter of
individual preference. It is desirable to have the two
hands overlapping, or at least touching; for the rest, the
player is well advised in holding the club in the manner
that he fancies. Do not, however, allow the hands to be
even a sixteenth of an inch apart on the shaft; the issue of
such separation is nearly certain to be fatal. Since I saw Mr
W. J. Travis play at Sandwich in 1904, I have always regarded his grip as theoretically the best one. So far as I can
remember, what he does is to overlap with the first and
second fingers of the left hand. He places those fingers
over the third and little fingers of the right hand. It might
be sufficient merely to put the forefinger of the left hand
over the little finger of the right. I have tried this kind of
hold, and done exceedingly well with it during periods of
respite from the agony of watching for that wretched

jump. If the reader will experiment with it, he will find that it very greatly reduces the danger of pushing the club away from the feet during the backward swing. It is one of the perils of putting that the right hand, which is essentially and naturally the putting hand, is apt to urge the club out in front instead of bringing it back in such a manner that it comes in a trifle towards the player. Mr Travis's grip seems to keep the right hand just sufficiently under control, and deter it from pursuing a wayward course. It may not suit all golfers, but in conception it is excellent.

The old maxim, "Never up, never in," is, I think, as valuable as ever. It is very easy to be too bold with the modern ball; but the man who is lacking in courage does not often win on the green. Nearly all good putters hit the ball with the utmost firmness. Watch, for instance, Tom Ball. He gives the ball a hearty (although none the less rhythmic) clout, and does not often fail. There are players who like to cut their putts. Jack White is, however, the only consistently good putter I know who invariably adopts this principle. The great mass of evidence suggests that the best spin is that imparted by the pull, which is produced by turning the right hand over in a very slight degree at the moment of impact. Willie Park, one of the finest putters I have ever seen, always pulls; so does Arnaud Massy, another deadly man on the green. Personally, I try to hit the ball without either cut or pull.

One cannot justifiably be dogmatic where putting is concerned, except in regard to the few points on which I have insisted. So many men, so many methods—that is the whole of the subject. J. H. Taylor, who is a most accurate putter and a rare man for holing the ball at a pinch, seems to me to have improved since he adopted his own particular style of sticking out his left elbow so that it points almost straight towards the hole as he makes the address and plays the stroke. His hands are well in front of the ball all the while. James Braid, who seldom misses anything that is holeable, has a way of stopping for quite a long while at the top of the putting swing. He takes the club back, and there he pauses for an appreciable period, as though he were coolly determining not to be guilty of a snatched shot. And the better he is putting, the longer he waits at the top of his swing. Every good putter possesses individualism.

Personally, I do not believe in studying the line from its two ends. The player who examines the situation first from behind the ball and then from behind the hole is likely to see two lines. He finds himself filled with philosophic fears and speculative doubts. The harvest that he reaps is so rich that he is distracted by it. He borrows a bit from one line and a bit from the other, and finishes where Fortune and a baffling complexity of slopes may take him. As I have said previously, there is a lot of imagination in seeing a line. In fact, it is nearly all imagination. If we take our "nightcap" in the form of ten minutes' putting in the dusk, we shall hole out with ease. We shall not see alarming undulations, which, the more we study them, the more they seem to demand infinitesimal estimation. We shall simply inspect the hole and the ball, and bring them close together. I sometimes think that with putts of a yard or four feet, it would be best if, without more than a cursory look at the line, we were to walk up to the ball and unaffectedly knock it into the hole. That is a counsel of perfection; it is just the system of George Duncan, and other wise appreciators of the difficulties of the short putt.

Putting is so much a matter of confidence that I sometimes think that the average player ought to be better at it than the champion. I say this with the knowledge that it looks remarkably like an excuse, but I believe that, when a man has a reputation to defend, the task of getting the ball into the hole from a comparatively short distance is more difficult than anything else in the game. In this connection I remember an incident that occurred at St Andrews a few years ago, when a tournament open to amateurs and professionals was decided. In the semi-final, Alexander Herd met an amateur, who holed putts from all parts of the green. The amateur generally had the worst of the play up to the green; then he would get down a long putt and leave Herd struggling for a half. The match was even at the seventeenth hole. At the eighteenth Herd won. Then he turned on his pertinacious rival. "Look here," he said, "you wouldn't hole the putts you've been holing to-day if you had to do it for your living." There was a lot of truth in that remark. Putting ought to be easy for amateurs; it is necessarily much more difficult for professionals, because their reputations are apt to depend upon it. Keep your head still, swing pendulum fashion with the arms and wrists, follow-through, and don't look up as you do it. These hints—and a recognition of the presumed fact that you are going to hole the ball—are the guides to happiness on the green.

PART IV
FROM "PROGRESSIVE GOLF"

CHAPTER I
FURTHER THOUGHTS ON PUTTING

FURTHER THOUGHTS ON PUTTING

I am not sure that there is any golden rule for achieving success on the putting green. A few well-defined principles there are that seem to have logic on their side, but they are only part of the constitution of that dispensation which we call deadly putting. The rest of the formula is a matter of individuality which cannot be communicated to anybody; it has to be born in a person.

I am far from suggesting that it is impossible to improve one's putting. Indeed, I know no detail of the game in which practice is of greater value. But that is mainly because it enables each player to discover for himself just what special characteristics he possesses in the business of laying the ball dead from a distance of twenty yards or holing out with certainty at a range of one yard—to learn how he is meant by nature to accomplish these tasks. Different golfers accomplish them in many different ways as regards their stances, grips, and methods of hitting the ball.

Putting is the department of golf which, more than any other, lends itself to experimentation and the exploitation of pet theories. So far as concerns the manner in which you stand, and the style in which you hold the club, and the sort of putter that you use (so long as they are not downright ridiculous), I am convinced that fancy may be allowed a fairly free rein. The all-important matter is to light upon a method that gives you the feeling that you are going to succeed, and then to practise it.

I doubt if any two people have precisely the same touch, which is a matter of supreme moment in putting. It represents the communication of the temperament and the nervous system in their most sensitive form to the act of striking a ball. Touch is of less account where the longer shots are concerned, because of the necessity of firm hitting.

In putting, it is delicacy in striking and a happy merging of caution into boldness in the mental attitude that pro-duces the desired effect. Some things—such as swaying the body during the movement of the club—are bad, but the question as to what is good opens up a wide field for exploration in which everybody can spend an interesting hour. What I would propose is that, when the player has discovered the method that gives him the greatest confidence, he should remain faithful to it unless it fails him long and badly at some later stage, and practice it for a quarter of an hour whenever he has the opportunity. In these periods he will learn much as to the strength that is required in striking the ball and the degree of "borrow" that is necessary on sloping greens—that is, if he pursues his studies, as he should do, on a green which boasts a certain amount of undulation.

Perhaps I need not remind the reader that my reputation as a holer-out is deplorable. How many short putts I have missed during the past fifteen or twenty years I should not like to estimate. They must number thousands. Once you lose your confidence near the hole, you are in a desperate plight, especially when you have a reputation to uphold and you know that a putt of two feet counts for as much as the most difficult iron shot. Nobody can say that a putt of this length calls for any real skill at golf; it simply demands confidence.

People who have seen me play tell me that my approach-putting is significantly better than average. So that perhaps I may, without presumption, offer a few hints on how to lay the ball by the hole from anywhere near the edge of the green. I am convinced that absolute stillness of the head and body is essential. One or two good putters there are who sway forward as they strike the ball, but they are such very rare phenomena as only to accentuate the importance to the ordinary mortal of the still head and body.

The stance may be that in which the player feels most comfortable, although I certainly do not believe in stand-

ing with the feet far apart. Rather would I go to the other
extreme, and have the heels touching. This, however, is
largely a matter of personal choice. If you keep the head
and the body absolutely still, and take the club back so
that it is not pushed outwards away from the feet but
inclines rather to come in slightly in the back swing, you
ought to hit the ball in a straight line. And that is obviously the first essential of successful putting. Judgment of
strength must come with practice.

When I was younger, I putted in a manner which was
really a concentrated form of what is known as the push
shot. I addressed the ball with the hands a little in front of
it, so that the face of the club was tilted over in a slight
degree on to the ball. As the club was a putting cleek with
a trifle of loft on it, this tilting over produced the effect of
a straight-faced club, and I simply came down on to the
back of the ball, and away it would speed with back-
spin—either to the hole-side or into the tin.

This principle suited me extremely well for years, but I
changed it ultimately in favour of a smooth, pendulum
swing; the arms moving backwards and forwards to
swing the club, and the head and body being perfectly
still. I think it is the soundest system; certainly it has
suited me remarkably well in playing all kinds of long
putts, and the reason I have missed so many short ones
has been mainly a tendency to lift the head with a jerk
through that "jump" which one experiences when one
fears suddenly that a shot is going wrong.

I am a whole-hearted believer in the overlapping grip
for putting. It promotes that unison of the hands which is
so important, for if you have the two hands working in-
dependently in ever so slight a degree in the delicate business of controlling a putt, the result is nearly sure to be
disastrous.

Examine the line only from the ball; never from the
hole. The confusion that results from studying the line

from both ends is embarrassing beyond words; whenever I have done it I have seen different lines, and that observed from the hole has proved to be the wrong one.

The bugbear of the short putt is, perhaps, that one is apt to exaggerate its difficulties. The longer one looks at it, the greater appear to become little undulations in the line, until in the end one tries to do cleverly by "borrowing" that which might be accomplished easily with a straight-forward, confident stroke calculated to send the ball firmly to the back of the tin.

Personally, I have made successful experiments at times—in public matches, it may be added—with left-handed putting. I have adopted this expedient when a right arm "jump" has been causing me to clutch the club extra tightly with the right hand the instant before the impact. Nearly every golfer has experienced this "jump" at some time or other; it is born of over-anxiety to do well, and is uncontrollable.

On the first occasion that I stood the wrong way round for putting—it was an exhibition match against, I think, Braid—I holed a putt of three yards. It is a very revolutionary remedy, but as half the bad putting is brought about by gripping too tightly with one hand or the other at the critical period of the stroke, almost any means of checking it is worth trying.

The overlapping grip discourages an unduly tight hold of the club, and, for that reason, it is a very good grip for putting, even in the case of golfers who do not like it when playing long shots. Tom Ball, an heretic on the subject of the pendulum swing, once related to me how he became converted to the overlapping grip.

On the eve of an important event, Ball was pumping the tyre of his bicycle when he ran the pump deeply into the fleshy part of the right hand, just below the thumb. He was anxious to take part in the competition, but he soon discovered that, with the ordinary palm grip, the pressure necessary with the right hand merely to enable him to keep control of the club caused great pain.

The overlapping grip, in the exercise of which the injured portion naturally rested upon the comparatively sympathetic flesh of the left thumb, afforded him considerable relief. He decided to employ it. He never afterwards abandoned it.

Ball had another story showing the efficacy of accidents as cures for golfing ills. When he was professional at the West Lancashire Club, near Liverpool, he often played with an esteemed doctor whose chief fault on the links was, in the opinion of Ball, that he jammed his right thumb too firmly on the handle of the club. He pressed so hard with it that, towards the top of the swing, the thumb and the club were apt to be fighting against one another.

The victim, however, seemed unable to rid himself of his vice. One day retribution overtook the thumb. Its owner ran a needle into it. He did not commit this act of malice aforethought on the principle that a desperate remedy might cure a desperate disease; it was an accident which caused him considerable annoyance at the time, since he had arranged to play golf on that very morning. He explained what he had done, and that he would have to give up the idea of going out for a round.

"Not at all," said Ball. "You've done the best thing in the world for yourself. You won't be able to press with the right thumb now." The lucky doctor went out and showed excellent form. And so happiness was brought to another soul.

Then there is the interesting case of Mr. Harold H. Hilton, who, at a time when the surgeon had forbidden him to play golf at all, accomplished what he has described as the best performance of his life. Most people who have studied the history of the game know that the rivalry between Mr. Hilton and the late Lieut. F. G. Tait was exceptionally keen. They met fairly often in various events, but for some strange reason their struggles nearly always ended in the discomfiture of Mr. Hilton. Only once did he succeed during the period in which Lieut. Tait occupied a position in the front rank of golfers, and that occasion was presented at the very time when Mr. Hilton was supposed to be nursing an injured hand.

The competition was for the St. George's Cup at Sandwich. The season was 1894. Some weeks before the meeting, Mr. Hilton badly tore the main sinew leading from the thumb and forefinger to the wrist. He was ordered by the surgeon to give up golf for a long while, and not to think of carrying out his idea of competing for the St. George's Cup.

Being as keen as he was human, he ignored the advice. From the time of the accident until he reached Sandwich, he did not use his injured hand; then he used it to such good purpose that he won. He was coupled with Lieut. Tait, and with a score of 167, the Englishman gained by three strokes the one and only sweet triumph over the favourite enemy.

In all these cases the players had to adopt a light grip, for the simple reason that their injuries prevented them from holding tightly, and I venture to say that they discovered something as to its merits, especially in putting. It is an involuntary tightening of the grip during the putting swing that causes the body to become rigid, and it is when the body is rigid that it is most likely to move.

I am sure that all my bad short putts—and they have been many—have been the result of moving the body, which has been the outcome of the right arm "jump" and consequent tightening of the grip.

Some very excellent putters—I would mention Willie Park and Arnaud Massy as examples—find that they obtain the best results, especially in playing long putts, by imparting a little "pull" to the ball. It is done by striking the ball nearer to the toe than the heel of the club-face; the mere act of following through in a rhythmic way secures the effect of "pull" so long as the impact occurs near the toe of the club. It is worth trying by the golfer who is inclined to "cut" his putts, for that, I think, is the worst thing possible with the modern ball, although Jack White used to practise it very effectively with the old ball. I place my faith nowadays in striking the ball with the middle of the club-face, swinging pendulum-like, and keeping the sole of the putter close to the ground throughout the swing.

Golf, for all the appearance of tame tranquillity that it is apt to present to the uninitiated mind, provides a more searching test of nerve and temperament than any other game in the world. That, indeed, is the opinion of most people who are experienced in the pursuit of sports and pastimes, and it is the cause of a phenomenon which offers much food for reflection. Golf is unique in the respect that it has two types of first-class players who are in the same grade so far as concerns the ability to hit the ball with complete skill and in perfect style, but who differ entirely in the results which they achieve in important events. One party can win championships, and the other party cannot for the life of it do anything of the kind. Yet to the person who has studied the methods of the less fortunate individuals, there seems at first blush to be no way of accounting for their failures.

In a comparatively minor competition or a practice round, they play in a manner which suggests that they are capable of succeeding in the strongest company and on any occasion. They execute the most intricate shot with ease and grace; it is impossible to be other than enthusiastic about their gifts. Somehow, when they make their efforts in classic tournaments, they prove deficient with a regularity that is distressing. To mention names would be invidious; every devotee of the game knows that there are truly great golfers who never secure championships and who exhibit such characteristics that, after a while, they are hardly so much as expected to win. Yet all the time they are recognised as brilliant players. Something is lacking in their nerve or temperament (the words, I suppose, are synonymous), and it is interesting to consider the various phases of this strange condition of affairs.

Personally, I am satisfied that in order to be a champion a person must have a good deal of sensitiveness in his nervous system. The man of sluggish disposition, the player with a truly "phlegmatic temperament" (that phrase which is so often used approvingly in regard to the individual who remains outwardly calm in a crisis) would not be likely to rise to greatness on the links. Of all games, golf is the one that comes nearest to being an art. It is pursued with deliberation and method; its inspirations are the player's own creation, since he is never called upon to strike a moving ball the action of which has been influenced by his rival. It demands the greatest delicacy and accuracy of touch, as well as the power to hit hard. An art requires a sensitive nervous system, and in golf the difference between the two sections of first-class players to whom I have referred is, presumably, that one can keep its nerves under control during the most trying period and the other cannot.

I have seen men positively trembling with excitement at the critical stage of a contest and yet possessed of such command over themselves as to be able to play every shot perfectly. This is just about as valuable a gift as the championship aspirant can possess, and to express surprise at a person's deficiency in regard to it is just about as reasonable as to be astonished at his inability to disperse a headache by will-power. For the great majority of people, it is in connection with short putts that nerves attain their most painful activity; there is nothing else in sport quite like the short putt at golf. You know that there can be no reasonable excuse for failing to knock a ball into a hole four feet distant, and yet there is a considerable chance of failing. And the higher the reputation of the player and the more, therefore, that is expected of him, the greater are the trials of the short putt. For all the skill that it requires, he has no advantage over the 24-handicap man, and he realises that, if he misses it, there will be no chance of recovery. It will be a hole lost or a stroke gone.

In all sincerity I express the opinion, after having undertaken three lengthy tours in the United States, that American golfers are better holers-out than British golfers. They are the cooler on the putting greens, and, after all, absence of anxiety is the chief essence of success.

Without doubt successful putting is mainly a matter of confidence, and that several great golfers fail to win championships by reason of their weakness near the hole is probably due to the fact that they have never gained complete confidence in their ability to get down a four-foot putt. For many happy years it did not so much as enter my head that I could miss a short putt, except as the result of carelessness; then I struck a bad patch in this hitherto simple business. The result was that there developed in my right forearm a nerve which puzzled a good many medical friends, and subjected me to indescribable mental torture. Whenever I prepared to play a short putt (it was only close to the hole that I had any trouble, so that the affliction must have been born largely of imagination and environment), I would wait for that nerve in the right arm to jump. The instant I felt it was about to start, I would make a dash at the ball in a desperate effort to be in first with the shot, and what happened as a consequence of this haste may be readily imagined.

Occasionally, the "jump" would leave me entirely for a month or two. Early in the final round of the Open Championship at Prestwick, in 1914, the wretched thing suddenly re-asserted itself. I felt the "jump" with a thrill of apprehension that is far from being a pleasant memory. Anyhow, the main point was not to let my partner and only formidable rival at that stage, J. H. Taylor, know anything about it. He was as well aware as I that if the distress became serious, I could miss putts down to six inches; it was strange to be walking along reflecting earnestly that not the smallest inkling of this development must be allowed to reach Taylor's ears, lest it should stimulate him to believe, as almost certainly it would have done, that he had me as good as beaten. Perhaps it was just this diversion from the thought of the possibilities of the jump itself that enabled me partially to overcome it and to struggle home first.

As a test of nerve, that last day's play at Prestwick was far and away the most trying I can remember. That we should have pulled ahead of the other competitors and then been drawn together for the final rounds was in itself sufficient to agitate either of us to the utmost; that we should have been struggling for the honour of a sixth victory in the championship (each of us, and also James Braid, having previously won five times) filled the cup of excitement to overflowing. I know that I played one shot without seeing the ball at all. It was buried in fine, loose sand, in a bunker to the left of the eleventh green, and close to the face of the hazard. The sand was scraped away from the top of the ball, but it was so loose that it closed over the object again. I simply could not wait; I swung, guessing and hoping, and fortunately hit the shot all right.

That was an exceptional occasion. In the ordinary way, I bear constantly in mind the conviction that the best way to win any important event is to play just as one would play a private round at home, and not endeavour to accomplish the performance of a lifetime. There is such a thing as trying too hard; it begets anxiety, which is usually fatal—especially in putting.

PART V
FROM "MY GOLFING LIFE"

I RETURN TO GOLF
AFTER MY ILLNESS

At the sanatorium in Mundesley the two things I was most fond of were barred. The doctors told me there was to be no golf and no smoking until I showed a good deal of improvement. If any incentive was required to make a rapid recovery, the thought of once again hitting a golf ball and puffing away at my beloved pipe was sufficient for me to make every effort to regain my accustomed health and strength.

My enforced rest cure was possibly more irksome than it otherwise would have been, owing to the fact that I had always experienced good health. I had, too, been extremely active. The thought that I would not be able for some time to lead my usual active life was depressing. However, I made the best of it.

After some months my health improved considerably, and I was able to leave the sanitorium early the following year. As it was still winter, I was advised to go to Le Touquet in France for a few weeks to get ready for the coming golf season. My stay at Le Touquet proved beneficial, and I came home in even better health. I was looking forward to defending my title as champion at Sandwich. Sandwich was one of my favourite courses and, in 1904, both the Amateur and the Open were held there. I think I am right in stating that this was the first occasion on which both these events were decided over the same course in the same year. Sandwich was to be the scene of another record. It was the first time the Amateur Championship had ever been won by an overseas competitor. This was the year of the sensational victory of Walter J. Travis, an American invader. When I was in the States four years previously, I had played against him and had seen sufficient of his golf to convince me he was a very sound player in all departments of the game. He was inclined to be somewhat short off the tee and through the green. However, his infinite capacity for taking pains and his wonderful putting had made a strong impression on me.

The Great Triumvirate: J.H. Taylor, James Braid, and Harry Vardon.

The Open Championship took place the week following Travis' historic victory. On this occasion, owing to the increased number of competitors, only eighteen holes

were played on each of the first two days. After a 76 on
the first day, I scored a 73 on the second and led the field
by three strokes. An indifferent 79 in the morning of the
concluding thirty-six holes spoiled what had appeared to
be a winning lead. With one round left, James Braid, with
a magnificent card of 69, was now leading with a total of
226. Jack White, too, had also improved his position and,
with a 72, was second—one stroke behind Braid. My total
of 228 placed me in third place, two strokes behind the
leader. With my brother Tom and Taylor standing at 229,
a close finish was anticipated.

Once again Sandwich was to be the scene of a surprising result. There were very few critics who thought Jack
White would be able to win. The general opinion was that
the Open would be won by a member of the Great Triumvirate, as Taylor, Braid and myself had been named a
year or two previously. For the last ten years, only two
other players had been able to win the Open. Although
White was a fine putter and iron-club player, it was
thought that his lack of length with his wooden clubs
might be too much of a handicap. Those who held this
view had not taken into consideration that the rubber-
cored ball had come into general use and that the course
was playing fast. These conditions helped a player who
was not capable of hitting the ball long distances. With the
rubber-cored ball, the Sandwich links was inclined to be
on the short side. The carries from the tee were not so
formidable as they had been in the days of the gutty.

Under these circumstances, there was nothing so surprising about White's success. He was accurate with all
his clubs, and he had for several years played awfully well
in the big tournaments.

In the concluding round some fine scores were made.
Jack White with a 69 was the first of the leaders to finish.
His aggregate of 296 seemed good enough to win. Both
Taylor and Braid made great efforts to equal White's total,

but failed by a single stroke. Taylor's score of 68 was a magnificent achievement, and Braid's two rounds of 69 and 71 constituted the lowest score for thirty-six holes in the history of the championship. I completed my final round in 74 and finished fifth.

Thus ended an historic two weeks play at Sandwich, with the two championships taking place on the same course and with the rubber-cored ball in general use for the first time. It was now clear to all that the gutty was doomed forever. A new era in the history of golf had arrived. In reflecting on these championships one is struck by the fact that both winners were comparatively short hitters and outstanding putters.

Soon after competing at Sandwich, I experienced a further deterioration in my health, but it was not of long duration, and again I made a good recovery.

In the 1905 Open Championship the following year, which took place at St. Andrews, I did not do well, finishing seventh. James Braid was the winner this year, his second victory in this competition. Later in the year I took part in one of the biggest events of my golfing life. This was the Great International Foursome which was played over four courses: St. Andrews and Troon in Scotland, and St. Anne's and Deal in England. J. H. Taylor and I represented England while James Braid and Sandy Herd represented Scotland. In foursome play, the two partners hit alternate shots and drive from alternate tees. No golf match in recent times attracted as much attention. It had been arranged that we should play thirty-six holes on each of the chosen links. The first portion of the match took place at St. Andrews. There was a huge crowd waiting for us, estimated at between ten and twelve thousand. Special trains from all parts of Scotland were run to St. Andrews for the event.

John L. Low was the referee, and Sir Thomas Parkyns and W. E. Fairlie acted as umpires. As in the case of my

match against Willie Park, flags were used to signal the
result of each hole. This was necessary so that the large
crowd of spectators would know how the game was pro-
gressing. A blue flag was raised when Taylor and I won a
hole, and a yellow flag when the Scotsmen won. When a
half was recorded, both flags were raised.

Beautiful weather favoured the encounter. Braid had
the honour of driving the first ball for Scotland, and Taylor led off for England. Chiefly by their skill on the putting
green, Braid and Herd forged a three-hole lead after the
first eighteen holes, but by the eighth hole of the second
round the match was square. There is no golf crowd in the
world more enthusiastic than those who follow a match in
Scotland. No single point is missed, and their apprecia-
tion of the fine points of the game is unmatched. As Scotland is the home of golf, its enthusiasts have witnessed
countless legendary matches. This would turn out to be
one of them. A fine putt by Herd at the tenth and a daz-
zling iron shot by Braid put the Scots three up once again.
The position looked serious for England when Taylor and
I lost the thirteenth. We won the next two holes only to
lose the sixteenth. At the Road Hole, Herd pulled his
second shot into one of the bunkers, and we won that
hole. A half in four at the eighteenth, and the first stage of
the match ended in favour of Braid and Herd, two up.

The second part of the Great International Foursome
took place at Troon on the following Wednesday, a day I
could hardly forget. When the day's play was completed,
Taylor and I had turned our two-hole deficit into an advantage of twelve, having won no fewer than fourteen
holes of the thirty-six. When one reflects on the sterling
golf produced by our opponents, it is difficult to understand how Taylor and I managed to win so many holes.
The golf of my partner and myself has been described as
some of the most remarkable ever witnessed. I would
have to agree. On many occasions we secured threes at

testing par four holes. I would drive, Taylor would follow up with his brassie or long iron, placing his shot within reasonable holing distance of the pin. This would enable me to sink the putt. On other holes the procedure would be reversed.

An outstanding feature of my own play were my cleek shots. At this period, my cleek was my favourite club, and I certainly did strike the ball accurately with it at Troon. Thus the second part of the contest was completed. Taylor and I were now in the happy position of being twelve holes up.

Arrangements had been made for the third part of the Great International Foursome to take place at St. Anne's in Lancashire, England, on September 6th. Golf is an unpredictable game. With our lead of twelve holes, the contest appeared to be basically over. At the conclusion of the day's play at St. Anne's, however, all that had changed. Nothing so sensational occurred as at Troon, but the Scotsmen had extricated themselves from an almost hopeless position. A spell of brilliant play on the part of Braid and Herd came as a serious check to the run of success which Taylor and I had had. It would be impossible to give too much credit to Herd for his brilliant putting which to a large extent gained for his side a victory of five holes on the day's play. Our opponents now had a sporting chance of pulling the game out of the fire.

The concluding stage of the Great International Foursome was played over the course of the Cinque Ports Club at Deal. Each side was out on the links the previous day for a practice round, and it was reported that the Scottish team had looked good. Taylor and I, too, were playing well. I had, with the exception of one or two slight lapses, been enjoying much improved health. Unfortunately, however, I was to experience a serious relapse the night prior to the match. My attack of haemorrhaging was so bad that Taylor did not think I would be fit enough to play

on the following morning, but when morning arrived I
was feeling much better.

We had been fortunate in having good weather
throughout the entire match up to this stage, but a bois-
terous wind was sweeping across the course accompanied
at intervals by drenching showers. We fought our way to
a six-hole victory during the morning round and so began
the afternoon round, the last eighteen of the contest, with
the overwhelming advantage of thirteen holes. It only
took six holes to end the match, with England victorious,
thirteen up with twelve to play.

Taylor and I had backed each other up admirably during the match. Whenever one of us made a mistake, the
other was able to come to the rescue. As far as my own
play is concerned, my cleek shots gave me the most satisfaction. One shot, in particular, stands out in my memory. This was at the sixth hole at Deal on the final afternoon round, the hole where the Great Foursome was
concluded. The length of the sixth hole is 259 yards, and
the wind was by no means favorable. I hit my tee shot so
well that my ball finished just over the green. This may
have been the best cleek shot I ever played in my life.

In 1906 the Open Championship was played at Muirfield. For some time before the event, the golfing critics
seemed to have decided that the Triumvirate, as Taylor,
Braid, and I were known, had finished its run of success
in the Open. In my own case, there may have been some
justification for this prediction. Aside from my troubled
health, I had finished a good many strokes behind the
leader the previous year. The general feeling was that I no
longer had the ability to win the championship. If this
were the case, I could at least reflect on my past record
with satisfaction. I had scored my first victory ten years
before, and from 1898 to 1903 could lay claim to having
been the best golfer in the field. I had won the champi-

onship in 1898 and 1899, finished second the next three
years, and won again in 1903. I had won the American
Open Championship in 1900. For another thing, winning
the big money match against Willie Park in 1899 was as
important to me as my Open victories.

The critics case against J. H. Taylor paralleled mine. He
had won the Open Championship in 1894 and 1895 and
had scored his third victory in 1900. Thus for five years
now he had failed to win. With Braid things were different. He had broken through in the Open in 1901 and had
won again in 1905 at St. Andrews, so that he was the
defending champion for the upcoming championship. In
addition to this, he had won two of the last three News of
the World match-play championships. The critics also
pointed out that there were several young golfers coming
to the front, most notably George Duncan, Ted Ray, and
Charlie Mayo. There was also the Frenchman, Arnaud
Massy. Massy was a topnotch golfer and, undoubtedly,
one of the finest putters of all time. Jack Graham and
Robert Maxwell were two amateurs who had winning
chances. I have always thought that Graham was an unusually gifted golfer, who possibly excelled at medal play
more than at match play.

The results of the 1906 Open, however, proved the critics entirely wrong as regards the Triumvirate. At the conclusion of the event, we occupied the first three positions.
At the end of the third round, everything had seemed to
point to another victory for Taylor. He held a three-stroke
advantage over Braid and myself. Graham, who took a 78
on the third round, was a stroke behind us. On the final
eighteen, Taylor and I started much earlier than Braid. I
spoilt my chances with a 78, and Taylor's indifferent 80
gave Braid the opening he needed to win his second consecutive Open, which he did by four strokes with a total
of 300. Braid is a strong competitor to put it mildly, and if
you give him a chance to win, he almost always takes

advantage of it. Taylor finished second at 304, and I was third, a shot behind.

The Open Championship of 1907 was held at Hoylake. This was to be the first occasion on which the Open trophy was gained by a foreign competitor. Arnaud Massy learnt his golf at Biarritz, in France, and was afterwards associated with Ben Sayers at North Berwick. He had already made a name for himself by his victory in the French Open Championship, which was played at La Boulie. Massy was possibly at his best under adverse weather conditions. The outstanding feature of his play, as I have said before, was his putting. He was nothing less than the best putter in the professional ranks. Massy used the same method of striking the ball as Willie Park. He played his putts with a slight draw.

In 1908, Massy defended his title at Prestwick. Braid walked away from the field and, with a total of 291, finished eight strokes ahead of the nearest man. I came in fifth after a disappointing performance. By his success at Prestwick, Braid had now scored his fourth win in the Open, equalling my own record.

Deal was to be the scene of the Open in 1909, the first occasion on which the championship had been held there. Taylor played outstanding golf throughout. His aggregate, 295, was made up of four steady rounds: 73-74-74-74. Braid was four strokes back. I was never in contention.

Additional interest was given to the 1910 Open Championship by the entry of Willie Smith, the famous Scottish-born professional, who at this period was located in Mexico. Smith led the field at the end of the first thirty-six holes with a total of 148, one stroke ahead of Braid. Duncan was third with 150. Willie Smith's second round of 71 was a record for St. Andrews. An 80 in his third round, however, put him out of the running. At this stage Duncan took the lead by tying Smith's record score of the previous day. His 71 gave him a two-stroke advantage

*Vardon, above, and Braid, below, tee off at St. Andrews in
the 1910 Open.*

over Braid. However, on the final round, Duncan fell away with an 83. Braid, with a 76 for 299, gained his fifth victory in the Open—moreover, his fifth in ten years. Once again, I was bitterly disappointed with my play.

Seven years had now elapsed since my last victory in the Open. It is true that after winning the championship for the fourth time at Prestwick in 1903, I had experienced a serious illness from which I was lucky enough to make a good recovery. However, there can be little doubt that my illness had left its mark on me. The chief source of my golfing troubles lay in the fact that I had become an indifferent putter.

In the days of the gutty ball, my putting was all that it needed to be. In fact, I can state that I was regarded as a good putter. It was interesting to read an article on this subject written recently by my old friend, J. H. Taylor, who states that, far from being a poor putter, I was, in my best days, one of the finest putters he has ever seen. While I make no claim to have been a great putter, I do think, in all fairness to myself, that I was not a bad one. The start of my fall from grace on the putting green was the result of my illness which, somehow or other, affected the nerves in my right arm. The rubber-cored ball, too, made me adopt different methods from those which I employed with the old gutty. With the gutty, it was possible—in fact, desirable—to strike the ball a firm blow. With the much livelier rubber-cored ball, a more coaxing stroke had to be employed. I am inclined to think that one of the reasons the nerves of my right arm were affected was my breaking a bone in my right hand while playing goalkeeper for the Ganton Football Club. This accident occurred after my return from my tour of the United States in 1900. The effect which my illness apparently had on the nerves of my arm may have been accentuated by a bone being out of place.

1911: CHAMPION AGAIN

Before the 1911 Open Championship, my old friend Arthur Brown and I went down to Sandwich and stayed at the Guilford Hotel. I had discussed with him the idea that a little light training on my part for the forthcoming event might prove beneficial to me. I came to the conclusion my method of training should consist of plenty of rest and a form of diet. I was convinced I would be more fit to tackle the strenuous conditions of the championship if I partook only of a light lunch. This was limited to some fish or a little chicken. I also made up my mind I would cut down on my smoking, but I did not give it up altogether. This, added to my resolve to retire at an early hour, constituted my training regimen.

Seven years before, in 1904, the rubber-cored ball had come into general use. By now it was well established and Sandwich, as a result, had undergone a few alterations and some lengthening. The one change which I personally regretted had the effect of making The Maiden, the renowned blind par-3 sixth, into just another hole.

Owing to the unusually large entry, the field had to be split up into three sections—A, B, and C. The A section played on the opening morning and the following afternoon. B played its rounds on the afternoon of the opening day and on the third morning, while C played on the second morning and third afternoon.

George Duncan led the field when the half-way stage was reached. His total of 144, made up of rounds of 73 and 71, gave him a four-stroke advantage over Ray, Taylor and myself. My play was encouraging, as my two 74s indicated, and my putting was better than it had been in the championships for the last few years.

I was one of the earliest of those in contention to start on the last day's two rounds. A stiff wind increased in strength as the day wore on. I started out playing very well, driving accurately and hitting my approach shots close. My putting continued to hold up, and I had a 36 on the first nine of my third round. I came back in 39, which gave me a satisfactory 75. It is the opinion of nearly all golfers that the third round in a championship is the most critical. I agree. The third round has far more bearing on the final result than is indicated by the scores. With the final eighteen holes coming up after lunch, I was the leader with 223. Taylor and Herd were second at 226, while Massy, Braid, Ray, and Duncan were bracketed together at 227. Harold Hilton, who shot 78, was one stroke further behind.

Apparently the light training I had undergone had had the desired effect, but I decided to have my lunch at the club instead of the hotel. I have no idea why I did this. If I had returned to the hotel, I would no doubt have stuck religiously to my diet, but instead I partook of a hearty meal, and this might very well have cost me the championship. In the final round, after reaching the turn in 38, I staggered home in 42 for an 80 and a total of 303 for the seventy-two holes. This gave several players golden opportunities to overhaul me. Since I had been one of the first players to tee off in the afternoon, all my rivals knew early in their rounds what it would take to beat me. Harold Hilton, for instance, had been five strokes behind me at lunch time, but by going out in a fantastic 33, he had pulled even. All he needed to do to beat my total was play the last three holes in thirteen strokes, and one of the last three, the 16th, was a short hole. Ironically, this was the hole that proved his undoing. His tee shot found a bunker. He played out of the bunker over the green, chipped back, and two-putted for a disastrous five. Fives on seventeen and eighteen gave Hilton a total of 304, a stroke higher than mine. Soon afterwards, Ray and Braid came down the stretch, each needing 75s to win, but both failed with 78s. The spotlight then fell on Sandy Herd. He arrived on the last tee needing a four to win the championship outright. Sandwich's eighteenth was a tough, testing two-shot hole, and in a crisis such as this, any golfer could be forgiven for failing to get his par. Sandy ruined his chance when he pulled his tee shot into the rough. He found his ball in a bad lie and was unable to do more than get it back to the fairway. His failure to reach the green with his third stroke cost him a six, and he finished in a tie with Hilton at 304.

The final climax was yet to come. Arnaud Massy needed a 75 to win. When he took 37 on the outgoing nine, things didn't look bright for him. However he started home faultlessly and, after holing out on the seventeenth green, was left with a four to tie. Massy now showed what a courageous golfer he was. Two full wooden club shots were needed to reach the green. His tee shot was perfect—straight down the fairway and long. A fine brassy got him on the green. Making no mistake with his putter, which he almost never did anyway, he holed out in two for his four and his 76, and tied my total of 303. Once again I was to be involved in a playoff for the Open Championship.

Sandwich had been the scene of an exciting finish in 1904, but I think the Open of 1911, with so many great players in contention on the last holes, will go down as having had one of the most thrilling climaxes ever. The tie between Massy and myself was played off over thirty-six holes the following day. I felt extremely fit as we teed off. Both of us played well on the first nine, and we were still level after the fourteenth. On the difficult fifteenth, I secured a four while Massy took a six. This was the turning point of the match. Massy had hung on with grim determination, but my four seemed to unsettle him. In any case, I quickly added to my lead, and by lunchtime I led by five strokes. I was playing the kind of golf I played in my prime: long off the tee, accurate with my brassy, sound with all iron clubs, and solid with the putter. In this playoff, I can truthfully say that my golf approached my old standards. In the afternoon, I reached the turn in 36 to Massy's 38, and by the fifteenth I had increased my lead to eleven strokes. On the seventeenth green, Massy, who had struggled gamely, retired from the contest. Once again I was champion.

The Open Championship of 1912 was held at Muirfield. When it is the turn of certain links to repeat as the scene of the Open, recollections of past championships there come vividly to mind. Muirfield had been the course on which I had gained my first victory in the Open, and, naturally, these links had pleasant memories for me. There were many alterations which had been made to suit the rubber-cored ball. Numerous bunkers had been added, and with the new linksland which had been incorporated into the course, Muirfield now had a more seaside aspect.

Before the event started many critics had predicted that Ted Ray would be a serious threat. His brother professionals, usually good judges of the form of their rivals, had also marked him down as dangerous. In the first round he returned a fine card of 71. A 73 gave him a total of 144, and he led the field at the half-way stage. I was quite satisfied with my own play. A 75 on the opening day and a really good 72 on my second round placed me second, three strokes behind the leader. Braid was third with a total of 148.

On the third day, Ray, with a 76, picked up five strokes on me and led me by eight. Braid and Duncan, who had been his nearest rivals when play started that morning, also lost ground to him. At this stage Ray held a lead of five strokes over the nearest man. With a good final round of 75 and an aggregate of 295, he was returned the winner of the 1912 Open. Ted's victory was very popular. He had proved himself to be a superior golfer, and he was a thoroughly good sportsman. He was a big hitter, capable of driving the ball prodigious distances. In fact, at this period, he was probably the longest driver in the world.

While speaking of long driving, it has always been difficult for me to understand why the run of the ball on the
ground is taken into consideration when records of long
drives are registered. In my opinion, the essential point is
the length of the carry, the determining factor in the days
of the gutty whose run on the ground could not approach
that of the rubber-cored ball. When the latter came into
general use, the carry was discounted and distance was
reckoned from the tee to the place where the ball came to
rest. How it arrived at its ultimate destination did not in
the least matter. As the rubber-cored ball lent itself to an
enormous run, golfers adopted a different method of hitting their tee shots. We became a nation of hookers, and
there is no doubt, in my opinion, that from this date a
depreciation in the golf of Great Britain started to set in.

In the autumn of 1912, the British Match Play Championship, the News of the World tournament, took place
over the Sunningdale course. At this time, Sunningdale,
especially from the extreme back tees and when the conditions were on the soft side, was a fierce test of golf. It
was also a wonderful course. There were some heroic
two-shot holes, and the greens were as perfect as a carpet.
The draw had placed me in the upper half which, as it
turned out, was the tougher half.

Rain fell continually throughout the first two rounds.
The luck of the draw had decreed that I should meet
George Duncan in the morning. Somehow or other, I felt
in advance that I would prevail. It was anticipated that my
match with Duncan would be hard-fought. A large crowd
saw me win— four up with three to play. I won, however,
only because I played exceptionally well. I was three under fours when the match ended.

In the third round on the second day, I faced Sandy
Herd. I recall vividly that we had an epic battle. Another
large crowd was around the first tee as we started out. I
reached the turn in thirty-six but found myself one hole

down. When Sandy increased his lead to two up with four holes to play, it appeared as if once again, after many close runs at the Match Play title, I was to be denied. However, a match is never lost until it is won, and I had not given this one up. I regained one hole at the fifteenth and drew level at the seventeenth. The gallery was roaring. Everything depended on the eighteenth. My drive was cut a little and finished a yard or two in the rough. Sandy hit one straight down the middle. Playing his brassie for his second, he appeared to "heel" it slightly, and his ball caught the bunker just short of the green. I also took my brassie and with a well-executed shot made the green. My opponent was not about to concede. He proceeded to play a marvelous recovery shot from the bunker and just failed to hole his putt and keep the match alive.

Ted Ray's path to the final had been relatively easy. So, too, was my semi-final match against a young star, Reggie Wilson. The final was close and dramatic, and the calibre of the golf very high. I remember it all as if it was yesterday. Ted Ray completed the thirty-six holes in 143 and yet was beaten. At last I had won this notable competition.

THE 1913
UNITED STATES OPEN

In 1913 I made my second trip to the United States through the good services of Lord Northcliffe. He had a house not far from my club in Totteridge, and suggested it would advance the interest in sport between America and Great Britain if we were represented in the forthcoming American Open Championship. He told me to choose a partner, for this would enable us to play a series of exhibition matches while there. I asked Ted Ray if he would accompany me. We decided to start on our tour directly after the British Open.

The Open was held at Hoylake that year, and J.H. Taylor, the winner, scored his fifth victory. By this success, J.H. tied with Jimmie Braid and me, each of us having won the Open five times.

Ray and I sailed from England at the beginning of August. It was now thirteen years since I had made my first trip to that great country. There were many friends I had made during my tour of 1900 with whom I had kept up a correspondence, and I was looking forward with great pleasure to seeing them again. I was also looking forward to taking part in the American Open Championship.

Throughout our trip both Ray and I played good golf. We took part in forty-one matches against the leading American players, and were defeated on only one occasion. I found the courses in America far better than they were on my first visit. All the same, I still felt that most of them needed a good deal of alteration before they could be reckoned as first-class.

The 1913 American Open Championship was to be held on The Country Club course in Brookline, Massachusetts. I believe there were one hundred and seventy competitors. Because of this huge entry, there had to be qualifying rounds, for which the competitors were equally divided over two days of play. One half completed their two rounds on the first day, while the remainder played their thirty-six holes on the second day.

We were favoured with fine weather and a large gallery when Tom McNamara, one of the leaders in American golf, and I set out for our first qualifying round. With scores of 75 and 76—151, I led the field in my section. Francis Ouimet, the young Boston amateur, was second, one stroke behind my total. Ray, with a total of 148 led the field on the second day in his qualifying section.

A tremendous crowd of spectators witnessed the play on the opening day of the championship. It was the general opinion of the officials that it was the largest gathering ever seen on a golf course in the country. Some good scores were handed in at lunch time: Macdonald Smith, 71; Walter Hagen, 73; Jim Barnes and Johnny McDermott, 74. I had a 75 which, with a 72 in the afternoon, tied me for the lead after the first two rounds with Wilfred Reid, another British player. Ted Ray had had a hard time of it in the morning and had taken a 79, but he came back in the afternoon with a sparkling 70, and his total of 149 was three strokes behind Reid and me at the halfway point. Ouimet had put himself into the picture with rounds of 77 and 74.

At this stage things looked bright for a British victory. The second and last day was to witness, however, a complete change. The weather deteriorated. In the morning it began to rain hard and never let up. I started out badly on my third round. A six at the opening hole and another six at the third was certainly not an auspicious start. I needed 41 strokes to reach the turn. I really did make a big effort on the second nine, and a 37 gave me a 78 for the eighteen holes. Ray with a 76 was tied with my total, and Ouimet with a 74 was also on the same mark.

The playing conditions on the final eighteen holes became even worse, but a player with my experience is used to competing in all kinds of weather, and I do not offer this as an excuse for my indifferent 79. I started out on my last round poorly again. In fact, I never remember record-

ing such high figures in an important event as I did on the
first five holes. Reaching the turn in 42, I came home in 37
for a 79 and a total of 304 for the seventy-two holes. Ray,
like myself, was an early starter, and he also recorded a
79, which gave him the same total as mine for the four
rounds. It appeared that both of us had thrown away our
chance of victory. There were several players battling
away who now had golden opportunities to defeat us, but
as player after player came in, soaked to the skin, and our
totals still stood untied or unbeaten, it began to look as if
Ray and I would have to play off for the championship on
the following day.

Later in the afternoon a rumour reached the clubhouse
that Ouimet was playing strongly and had an outside
chance of winning the championship. We decided we
would go out and see for ourselves exactly what was happening, and we witnessed the last four holes which the
young American played in such dramatic fashion. He had
to play these four holes in one under par to tie us. He got
his pars at the fifteenth and sixteenth. At the 360-yard
seventeenth, he hit his second shot about ten yards from
the pin. He then holed his putt for a three. He had picked
up the stroke he needed, and now if he could par the
difficult eighteenth, he would tie for the championship.

The eighteenth is a long par 4 to an elevated green
bunkered in front. Ouimet played it well, leaving himself
a five-foot putt for his par. He stroked the ball into the cup
and created a triple tie. I would like to state that this was
one of the most courageous exhibitions of golf in a national championship I have ever witnessed. The tie between Ouimet, Ray, and myself was played off on the
following morning over eighteen holes. I think it was a
mistake to decide such an important event by the outcome
of one round. There is no doubt that good or ill fortune
plays a fair part in the outcome of all sporting contests,
and the luck of the game usually equalizes itself, but I

The eighteenth green: the playoff of the 1913 American
Open. Ouimet, on the left, lines up his putt. Vardon and
Ray wait.

think that in golf it may easily require more than a round
of eighteen holes.

The morning on which the playoff was to take place
was as wet as the previous day. During the entire round
the rain never stopped for a moment. There was a tremendous gathering of spectators at the first tee as we set
out. We all played steadily on the first nine, each of us
scoring thirty-eight. I continued to play well on the homeward nine, and, when the fifteenth hole had been con-

cluded, I had a three-stroke advantage over Ray. It was a
shock to realize that at this stage Ouimet was one shot
ahead of me. I must now make something in the nature of
a confession. I had started out with the preconceived idea
that, if I defeated my fellow-countryman, I should win the
championship. It must not for a moment be thought that
I underestimated the capabilities of Francis Ouimet. I had
seen sufficient of his golf on the previous day to realize
how good he was, but I did not think he would prove able
to sustain that form in the playoff. I had made a mistake.
The seventeenth hole decided the event. I was bunkered
off the tee and took a five. Ouimet was on the green in
two and, for the second day in a row, holed a sizeable putt
for a three. I proceeded to play the home hole in an indifferent manner and took a six. Ouimet finished with a
perfect four which gave him a 34 for the last nine and a 72
for the round. He had proved himself to be a superior
golfer and a courageous fighter. My own score was 77,
one stroke ahead of Ray.

Ouimet's great victory would prove in the years ahead
to be a decisive factor in the advancement of golf in the
United States.

MY SIXTH VICTORY IN
THE BRITISH OPEN

Many people who saw me play during the year 1914, were convinced I was playing at the level of my great years—1898, 1899 and 1900. I do think that in a few tournaments this was the case, and one of those tournaments was certainly the 1914 Open at Prestwick. This was not only one of the highlights of the year but of my whole golfing life. Of all the head-to-head duels I have had during my career, my battle with J.H. Taylor on the final two rounds of this Open must be considered in a class by itself.

The crowd that final day was enormous. There were nearly five thousand people following us in the morning round. In the afternoon, this figure must have doubled. Special trains kept arriving from Glasgow and other places bringing additional spectators. As a matter of fact, there were far too many people on the course. It was an experience I would not care to go through again. I wonder if the average golfer has the slightest conception of what a player undergoes under such conditions. He is battling to win the greatest championship in his profession. Seventy-two holes of medal play is a severe test of skill and nerve to begin with. The addition of an enormous and wild crowd doubles the difficulty. In an effort to have a good view of each stroke, the crowd swarms and surges, and the players are buffeted and knocked about. It may come as a surprise to people to know that, after a big tournament, my ankles and shins are black and blue. The moment I have struck my ball, it is absolutely essential for me to give my club to my caddie to prevent it from being broken by the rushing crowd. As I walk along in the midst of this multitude, I am pushed, elbowed and kicked. Under these circumstances, trying to produce one's best golf calls for incredible concentration and self-control.

There is another reason why this championship was to prove to be one in a hundred. Braid, Taylor, and I had all won five Opens. Winning the sixth might clearly establish which of the three of us had the upper hand. Thus when Taylor and I, the two leaders, were drawn together on the last day for the concluding thirty-six holes, it was a moment of high drama.

Prestwick was a very different course than it was six years previously when it had last hosted the Open. Back tees had been installed at many holes. The ninth and tenth each played forty yards longer than they had before. Over five hundred yards had been added to the course, which stretched to upwards of six thousand, five hundred yards. In addition, a large number of new bunkers had been created.

Vardon at Prestwick in 1914. Forty-four years old, he won his sixth Open.

It was a truly marvelous golf course and one, I should add, which contained many of my favorite holes. The third, known as the Cardinal, is one of the finest long holes in the world, measuring four hundred and ninety-two yards. A straight tee shot is required if the famous bunker, after which the hole is named, is to be carried with the second stroke. The green is long and narrow, and any player getting home in two may well be satisfied with both his length and his accuracy. The fifth is a blind one-shot hole of one hundred and ninety-six yards called Himalayas. The Himalayas is the high ridge of sand that must be carried to reach the green. Number nine, Eglinton, at four hundred and ninety-three yards, played exceptionally hard in this championship. Many new bunkers had been added, and anyone avoiding these hazards with his second shot not only had to be very accurate but had to have a bit of luck as well. On the homeward journey, the eleventh, Carrick, and long twelfth, Wall, are challenging, while the fifteenth, Narrows, a hole of three hundred and twenty-five yards, is diabolically narrow off the tee, as its name implies. The seventeenth, the Alps is in my opinion the greatest golf hole in the world. A long straight drive is necessary if the player is to be in a good position for his second shot, which has to be played over an enormous ridge to an unseen green. It is a hole with a great history.

I set out on that memorable final day with a lead of two over my longtime rival, Taylor. The third round in a championship is the critical one. On this occasion it was also a thrilling one. At the turn I led him by three strokes.

Taylor is well known for his sterling fighting qualities. I had played with him on so many occasions that I was well aware of this. Never were these qualities more in evidence than in the third round at Prestwick. J.H. found more than his fair share of trouble during the early morning. Then he turned the tables. Three behind at the end of the

Taylor picks up another stroke on the first green in the final
round of the 1914 Open at Prestwick.

first nine, he gained five strokes on me on the second
nine, and I did not in any way play badly!

I don't recall ever playing a shot where I couldn't see
the ball, but it happened on that disastrous nine holes.
My tee shot on the short eleventh, Carrick, found the
bunker. My ball was so completely buried that at first we
were unable to find it. Eventually it was located, and John
Laidlay, who was acting as umpire, had to scrape some of
the sand away in order to see the top of the ball. As soon
as this was done, the fine sand immediately closed over it
again, and I played this stroke more with a sense as to
where the ball was located than actually knowing its exact

position. It was disheartening coming as it did when my lead was fast disappearing.

My recollections of the afternoon final round are still vivid. The spectators formed an almost solid wall from the left of the first tee to the hill in front of the first green as Taylor, who was leading by two strokes, drove off. The excitement was intense and it was obvious that my opponent and I were in for a long and trying ordeal. It was essential for me not to dwell on Taylor's shocking surge in the morning. I reminded myself that I was playing well, that I had a fair chance of winning, and that I must concentrate on making as few mistakes as I possibly could. Additionally, after Taylor's heroics in the morning, it was not unreasonable to think he might drop a shot or two during the afternoon. His effort must have taken a good deal out of him.

At the opening hole, however, Taylor increased his lead to three. The first hole, Railway, was unusually difficult because the ground was so dry and hard that it was almost impossible to stop a pitch on the green. Mine trickled over it. I ended up with a six and lost a stroke to Taylor's five.

It has been generally held that my opponent lost the championship at the fourth hole, where a series of disasters resulted in his finding the creek, Pow Burn, and taking a seven. I personally have always held the opinion that the third hole was a more important factor than is generally realized. We had halved the short second, which brought us to the famous Cardinal with Taylor still leading by three strokes. There, after a solid drive, I hit my brassie onto the green close to the pin. Taylor did not get home in two and took a five. I missed my putt but had an easy four, and was now only two strokes behind. I remember clearly that the two shots which I played at the Cardinal that afternoon gave me the confidence I needed to still win this match.

My opponent's experience at the fourth, where he got into the burn which runs along the right side of the hole and ended up taking a seven, was a shock from which he never seemed to recover.

I gained another stroke at the Himalayas and, at the turn, held an advantage of three strokes. From the second to the ninth I had run off seven consecutive fours. On the last nine I continued to play sound, steady golf and gave my opponent no opportunities to reduce my lead. With three holes left to play, I led by five shots. On the sixteenth, Cardinal's Back, Taylor had a three, while I took a five. Taylor never gives up. We both finished with two fours. My total for the championship was 306, three strokes better than Taylor's.

When I had holed my last putt I felt so tired and exhausted that all I wanted to do was to sit down and rest.

I have been asked at different times if there were any outstanding features of my own play during that Open which impressed me particularly. If there was one thing, it was my play with my wooden clubs. I do not think I have ever driven better than I did on the opening day of the championship. I was hitting a very long and accurate ball from the tee. Above all, three brassie shots I played linger in my memory. When I was at my best, this club was a great favourite of mine. These three shots vividly recalled the old days. Two of them were played at the same hole, the Cardinal. One was on my opening round and the other on the final eighteen. The third was my second stroke to the long ninth on the third round, when I placed my ball not far from the hole. I think many other people remember that shot.

1920: MY LAST AMERICAN TOUR

Ted Ray and I had at the conclusion of our 1913 tour in the United States promised to pay another visit. We decided we would go soon after the 1920 British Open Championship. I wrote to Alec Finlay and asked him if he would represent us as manager. He advised me to get in touch with A. Peterson, who was a well-known golf architect. Peterson had offices in different parts of the country and did a big business in Carter's seeds. It was arranged that he should look after our interests in the east, while in the west we would have another manager. We again had a very enjoyable but extremely strenuous trip. At one period we travelled for six straight weeks and never slept in anything but a railway sleeping car.

After seven years I again found a big change in the attitude of the Americans towards the game. In 1913, there had been a few promising homebred golfers, such as J.J. McDermott, Jerome Travers, and Chick Evans. Now there were a great number who appeared headed for notable golfing careers. Unless Great Britain was able to produce some fresh blood to take the place of the old-timers, our supremacy in the royal and ancient game would be seriously challenged.

During my previous visit I found that it was the tendency of the players in the United States to indulge in an excess of wild swiping. They were to a great extent a nation of hookers. Their courses required considerable alteration. Their design did not emphasize that basic element of tournament golf: the skill to keep the ball in the fairway. Now, seven years later, I found all this changed. The courses had been vastly improved, and it was now necessary to drive both accurately and long if good scores were to be had. Golf, in short, was not only booming but the level of skill on which it was being played had risen dramatically.

We began preparations for the American Open Championship to be held at the Inverness Club in Toledo, Ohio.

Vardon, fifty, was paired with Jones, eighteen, in the qualifying rounds at Inverness in 1920.

I had turned fifty, and I realized it would be more difficult to survive the rigors of a championship. Despite this, I thought I had an excellent chance of winning the United States Open. One reason for this confidence was that I was playing my cleek well and could hit it with my old authority.

In both qualifying rounds at Inverness, I was paired with Bobby Jones. Although only a young man of eighteen, he had proved his mettle by reaching the final of the U.S. Amateur Championship the previous year. With his fine natural swing and good control, his golfing future certainly appeared to be bright. Apparently, he needed a little more time to get his temper under control.

I was pleased with my two opening rounds of 74 and 73. These scores were equalled by Ray, and our total of 147 placed us in third position. Jock Hutchison, who was attached to the Glen View Club, was the leader at the halfway mark with 145.

In the third round I had a 71 and was leading the field with 218. Hutchison and Leo Diegel were a stroke behind. Ray was one shot further away. If I had been able to win the 1920 American Open, I would have considered it one of the outstanding performances of my golfing life. For over thirty years I had been one of the leaders in the game. Upon occasion, I was capable at fifty of playing as well as I ever had.

I started my final round in fine style, and when I reached the turn it looked as though I was going to win. With seven holes left to be played, I was still in front. At this point a tremendous gale off Lake Erie swept across the course. Under ordinary circumstances these conditions would not have made that much difference. I was tiring fast, however, and having to fight my way through such a storm required more stamina than I possessed.

I dropped stroke after stroke as hole succeeded hole. On checking my score after the round, I could scarcely

Vardon, in top form, in the 1920 American Open at Inverness.

believe I had taken 78 strokes, particularly when, with only seven holes to play, I was one stroke under even fours for the championship. To finish as I did was a crushing disappointment.

I was genuinely happy that my fellow-Jerseyman, Ted Ray, an old and good friend, brought in a 75 on that punishing last round and won the championship by a stroke.

As I look back on my third visit to the United States, it is with a feeling of pride and satisfaction that I witnessed the enormous popularity which golf had gained in that great country. In 1900, the game had been in its infancy. Now, in 1920, it was the national craze. The skills of the players, I might add, had increased commensurate with the game's popularity. I think in my three visits I helped sow the seeds of all this.

There was little question in my mind that the time was not far distant when the British Open Championship would be won by an American golfer.

Ray and I had experienced a successful trip in every way. Our exhibitions had been well received, and we had been given further proof of the justly celebrated American hospitality. It was a fitting climax to our tour to have the honour of bringing home the American Open trophy which my partner had so gallantly won.

Afterword
by
S. L. McKinlay

Harry Vardon was sometimes described as the Jersey Greyhound. The sobriquet neatly embraced his place of birth, his graceful elegance of action, and his ability to outdistance his pursuers. To me, however, his name always brings to mind another animal, a horse. But no ordinary horse—a winner of the Epsom Derby no less.

Let me explain. In 1919 the Glasgow Golf Club, of which I later became a member, promoted a Victory Tournament in place of the Open Championship to celebrate the ending of World War One, or the Great War, as we knew it. All the leading professionals were invited to take part in a match-play event over three days on the club's city course at Killermont, five miles from the city centre. They included the Great Triumvirate, Harry Vardon, James Braid, and J.H. Taylor; the young lions, Abe Mitchell and George Duncan; Arnaud Massy, from France; and one or two oldsters, such as Wee Ben Sayers and Andrew Kirkaldy.

It happened that at the time I was not at school because of a minor eye ailment. Reading was forbidden, but that was the only limitation. My father, himself an ardent and capable golfer, thought it would be salutary for me to see some of the masters in action, so I was despatched, eagerly but apprehensively, on the morning of June 5 to make my way by tramcar right across the city to Killermont, quite an adventure for an 11-year-old in short trousers.

When I arrived on the first tee I found myself standing beside two bowler-hatted city businessmen just before Vardon took the tee for his match. Their conversation was animated, and I assumed they were golfers discussing the prospects for the day's play. How wrong I was. The conversation went this way: "I can't see anything beating The Panther. He's not the favourite for nothing." "Rubbish. Take my tip. Back Lord Glanely's Grand Parade—it's the only real dark horse in the race." At which point Vardon stepped on to the first tee and into my heart as my first golfing hero. Oh, I ought to add that Grand Parade did win the Derby that day, and at 33 to 1. As I think Mr. Runyon put it, "You can look it up."

Vardon looked the part—well dressed in tweed knickerbockers and jacket, cloth cap, and well-polished brogans. When it was his turn to play, he perched his ball on a twist of damp sand (no peg tees in those days), took the most comfortable stance it was possible to imagine, grinding the turf with his right foot to make sure his hobnails were gripping. A few waggles, and off went his drive right to the heart of the green, 270 yards away. The swing was elegant, the shot was perfect, golf looked to be the simplest activity in the world, and altogether much more exciting than weighing up the prospects of a horse race to be run 400 miles away.

Alas, that is almost the sum of my memories of my first encounter with the great men of golf. I did see Braid play a towering mashie shot to the short sixteenth hole that I tried to emulate every time I played the hole in the nearly fifty years of my membership. I saw Duncan, who was the Prince of Darkness among the pros, slash his drive through the first green into an evil place from which he recovered with insolent insouciance. He went on to win the tournament, demolishing J.H. Taylor in the final by 6 and 5 to win first prize—fifty pounds, a fistful of dollars.

But the memory of Vardon was important because later that year I was on holiday at Millport, a seaside resort on the island of Cumbrae in the Clyde estuary, with a splendid sporting course on the top of the island. In the tin-roofed clubhouse, where I spent every waking hour when I was not playing golf, there was a copy of Vardon's "The Complete Golfer." I was by that time able to read again, and on several wet days of my holiday I devoured Vardon. I can remember the photo of the nine clubs he used in winning his first four Open Championships. I patterned my driving stance on his, as set out in a wonderful pho-

tograph showing Vardon standing on a dark surface on which white tapes formed a grid.

He was the greatest golfer of his age. P.G. Wodehouse recognized this in selecting him as one of the two British professionals that the Russian golf nut venerated in "The Clicking of Cuthbert": "Arbmishel and Arreevadon." Sadly, Abe Mitchell, Britain's Sam Snead, never won the Open title that he deserved.

Of course, Vardon was given credit for inventing the grip that bears his name, in which the little finger of the right hand rides on the forefinger of the left, in order to keep the hands together. But the true inventor was an amateur, and a very good one, too, J.E. Laidlay, who, like Vardon, had very large hands. Vardon's were enormous. Someone once said that he looked as though he were carrying a bunch of bananas in each hand. Just how big they were I realized when I placed my own hands in the mold of his grip made by an enterprising rubber manufacturer—a cast of his grip that was supposed to be fitted to the clubshaft.

Vardon remained my hero for a year or two until he was superseded by, of all people, George Duncan, who was the exact opposite of Vardon in style, demeanor, dress—in everything, in fact, except accomplishment. But Duncan finished 3 3 to win a big-money tournament on the Old Course at St. Andrews, and anyone who could get a 3 at the Road Hole was a hero to me. Oddly, Duncan influenced his fellow-professionals a good deal; he was regarded as the pros' pro. Vardon, an infinitely finer technician, never seemed to exert the same influence. There was no Vardon school of golfers. He was admired as a player, of course, but not, I think, copied except by romantic schoolboys like myself. Maybe his style was too individual. He had a very upright swing, he held on to the club with both hands in a manner equalled only by his devoted admirer Henry Cotton, who, however, contrived to have a straight left arm at the top of his backswing whereas Vardon's was notably bent. Perhaps Vardon's most valuable contribution was that he set standards of excellence that forced his contemporaries into agonies of emulation.

It used to be said of Vardon that direction flags were hazards to him because he hit the ball so straight, and that if he played two rounds in a day he sometimes had to play his second-round second shots from the divots he had taken in the morning. Poppycock, of course, but rather an appealing way of exaggerating the straightness of his hitting. He was one of the genuinely great golfers, a true thoroughbred like the animal that won the Derby on the day I saw him in all his elegance.

S. L. McKinlay